The Soul of a Christian Nation

WEEPING

The Soul of a Christian Nation

WEEPING

ROBERT A. LITTLE

ARPress
ILLUMINATING IDEAS
EMPOWERING MINDS

ARPress
45 Dan Road Suite 5
Canton MA 02021
Hotline: 1(888) 821-0229
Fax: 1(508) 545-7580

Ordering Information:
Quantity sales. Special discounts are available on quantity purchases by corporations, associations, and others. For details, contact the publisher at the address above.

Printed in the United States of America.

ISBN-13:   Softcover   979-8-89330-894-5
                  eBook   979-8-89330-896-9
                  Hardback   979-8-89330-895-2

Library of Congress Control Number: 2024902583

Table of Contents

PREFACE : I

INTRODUCTION : V

Chapter One : Old Testament 1

Chapter Two : New Testament 27

Chapter Three : After Crucifixion 52

Chapter Four : Christianity in Early America 67

Chapter Five : Christianity in Todays Society 101

Conclusion : 160

PREFACE

I started this book over four years ago, when President Trump took office, prior to his winning the 2016 election, At the time he made comments and exhibited behavior that deeply troubled me. As his Presidency continued, many persons wrote books about how they were personally, affected or offended. I originally started down the path of writing specifically about Trump and his far right followers. I decided instead, to write about how he should be offending Christians or the reason why he is not offending them. As the years grew, I just kept writing. I viewed Trump's twisted policies as a product of and the results of Far-Right and Evangelical thinking. Then I realized that in spite of Trump's repeated behaviors, which were in direct opposition to Christianity and the Bible, he was a product of this great country. His mindset, morals and disregard for equality and the principles of decency were actually a part of this country's history, present and possible future. His behavior is a direct correlation of the views of just at least half of the population of America. Our laws and Constitution provided the means of acceptance and continued behavior. No one posed the fact that is was anti-Christian. Contrarily those who opposed where call anti-Christian. That is a problem with our country

After over three years I pinpointed my objective. To write a book, which focuses on the cause and effect of religion and our country's foundation.

This includes the lack of morality, and the lack of love this country shows its citizens of all races, religions, ethnicity, gender and social status.

I could pick particular points in our history, but many people would ignorantly justify the despicable behavior with the Bible or the Constitution. Therefore, I decided to go back to the beginning. Not the beginning of our country's founding, but back to Christianity itself. Is there a correlation between what God speaks in the Old Testament, what Jesus speaks in the New Testament and the founding, growth and direction of our great Christian nation?

I submit that at this particular point in our lives, we see what institutions, what religions and what type of people are proponents of spewing insensitivity, racism, bigotry, gun violence and overall inequality. We blame the institutions of society. We blame the Far Right. To be honest, so do I. Many blame the Far Left. We blame the government as a whole, along with the video games and poor educated citizens. There is no more need to rehash what we already know. No need. My attempt in these pages is to uncover the root cause and analysis. So, I asked myself. Do I focus on one political party, one president or maybe a certain economic group? I first chose to focus on Trump, then the far right evangelical thinking crew. As the years passed by – because that is how long I have been writing this – I realized the problems our country faces are inherit, systemic and engrained in everything we hold dearly. The views of Donald Trump, his base, those afraid to be virtuous human beings and the millions of other prejudice, selfish, racist, egotistical people, are the views of millions, which began thousands of years ago. The moral dilemma we are faced with is actually centuries old. As old as religion.

We have been taught and grown to believe that the history of our country is defined by good, up-standing, God-fearing men. History has shown that not all heroes or good Samaritans are religious and certainly not Christian. But, they all have something in common. They care about their fellow man, they care about the future generations and they care about humanity. So, I would submit that whether it is accepted or not, those who are good at heart share that one thing in common. And those who only care about themselves and disparage others in the human race also, have something in common. But how do we explain this? Do we determine or define character based on political beliefs? On religious beliefs? On social stature? Let us break it down.

INTRODUCTION

There have been many books, memoirs, biographies and autobiographies written in the past few years about what was felt by people who were offended and even honored by the actions of our former administration and all administrations to be exact. Most are aimed at identifying the behaviors of a particular person or group. As previously mentioned, I have been torn, conflicted and just baffled at what approach I would take in my attempt to get my point across. Well what is the point of this book? I sway back and forth. Is it political, religious or just food for thought? Maybe all of the above.

This book is for all those who love God and seek Him. It is for all those who love God in public and those who worship Him in private. Those who go to church and those who do not. Those who believe in the Bible and those who have let the world's inhumanity cause them not to believe in the Bible or any other original spiritual doctrine. This book is for those who profess to be Christians, and those who are really Christians; whether Catholic, Protestant; whether Methodist, Evangelical, Baptist, Lutheran, Jehovah's Witness or any other denomination. The Christian right and Christian left. This book is also for all those who have turned away from Christianity because of the hypocrisy of Christian scholars, leaders and self-proclaimed men of God. This book is for those who love God but are not sure about the existence or deity of Christ. It is for those who may not believe in the practice of religion at all. And this book is for all, in all nations, who believe in their hearts that America is truly a Christian nations… and for all those who feel America is not. For some this book will confirm their understanding of God. For others it may confuse them, but lead them to further study the scriptures, in order to validate the writings in this book. And for others it will simply piss them of… hopefully. Many readers may wonder why I am focusing on Christianity. To be honest I could apply this to countries whom profess to represent other religions. Jewish states or Islamic states. Even though these days, I would rather use the term Muslim countries. The topic for this book is America and therefore Christianity.

This book contains facts. It is not propaganda. It is not fake news. There is no agenda, but my personal knowledge and observations. This book is not about perception or subjectivity. Mine or anyone else's. This book is about the truth as told by the Bible. As well as truth represented in our country's founding documents. This book represents objective, irrefutable facts; from the Bible, from scholars, from academia, from historical documents and linguistic definitions. It is not about proving anything, but about understanding. Why am I focusing on the Bible? Because so many politicians, so many holy rollers and so many hypocrites use Christianity as a badge (though plastic) of honor. I hear people campaigning on their strong Christian beliefs. I listen to people embellish their vanity based on their knowledge of two Bible verses. So I thought I would point out a few things for all those who profess they live a Christian life. I struggled as to how I would approach this. I certainly do not want to come across preachy. That would defeat the purpose, and frankly there is too much of that now. Plus, I am not worthy of preaching to anyone. So forgive when I do get preachy.

A few years back, a "What would Jesus do" phenomena, waved through America. It seemed to awaken the Christian values Jesus taught, but soon became nothing more than a fad. An esoterically, empty question which did not place value on spiritual things but more on the ritualistic trophy mentality of displaying words which said, "hey look I am a Christian" We should have probably been posing that question throughout the history of our great nation. A nation which proudly taunts the Christian values or the Christian symbols it wears proudly in its own mind. A nation whose purpose is to proudly proclaim it exist to fulfill the legacy of Jesus Christ.

If you believe in Jesus, do you think he is proud of his legacy? And for all those who do not believe in him, but are aware of what he is claimed to have taught and what Christians are supposed to stand for, do you think he would be pleased? Before we address that question we must understand what he stood for, what he wanted his followers to teach others, and how he wanted his fellow man to live. The answer to these things lay in the foundations, not of religion, but in the foundations of spirituality. Let me start at the beginning.

Man. No one really knows how long this being, mammal, homosapien has wondered the Earth. Some believe only 3000 to 5000 years. Some also believe the pandemic was a hoax. Some people believe anything they read on Facebook. Not everyone agrees on how Man even came to exist. Some believe evolution spawned modern man. Some believe Adam was the first man who walked the earth. And if you do believe Adam was the first man, then we will view that briefly a little later. Few will argue that since the dawn of man, spirituality and worship has been part of man's being. The belief in a Supreme Being is what many say, separates man from other living beings whom inhabit this planet. Some may say intelligence, but that is equally arguable. Some say spirituality. There are those that replaced spirituality with religion. And that is where things get sticky. According to old scripture engravings and text, man's spirituality and worshiping of a Supreme Being can be traced to the dawn of man, to the dawn of time, to the "beginning". As time progressed man's view points and beliefs matured (supposedly) and his knowledge of a Supreme Being grew (so I've been told). Then something in history changed. Spirituality transformed into religion, and religion transformed into politics, segregation, and domination. Many different religions sprouted throughout the world. Christianity, Islam, Judaism, Hinduism and Buddhism, to name a few. All claiming to be the true religion that man's Supreme Being represented. The truth that was once loved, honored, respected and even feared. Among all the religions, none of them has had the impact on world history, as did Christianity. We must realize that back years and years ago, there were many forms of spirituality and many spiritual people. We also must understand Jesus' disciples started the first true religion as defined today. Christianity, in its present form, is a religion that began over 1600 years ago (though many say 2000 years) and has shaped values, traditions, politics and international alliances ever since it was formally established. I say 1600 years because Jesus taught what we should learn and follow, but is was not for many years that the actual religion came into existence. What Jesus taught is my definition of what Christianity should be. In this book I am talking about the Christianity that has shape our world today. The "religion" of Christianity. Unfortunately, it has also spawned the justifications for wars, genocide and other acts of inhumanity. And again, this is not subjective or an opinion.

Over 1 billion people worldwide profess Christianity. The optimum word being professes. Because someone says they are a Christian, recites a few Bible verses or holds up a Bible does not, in anyway, mean they are a Christian or any other religious affiliate. Those who believe, use sacred documents to prove that this religion was one born of God Himself. But, from the very beginning, that is after the death of Jesus Christ, there have been those who defined, practiced, taught and even enforced different views of Christianity than those before them and of their fellow family members. They subsequently molded our modern day Christianity. Why? What are the different interpretations of those sacred documents, which were compiled to create the Bible? How did man and the so-called self-proclaimed prophets teach the Bible? Now I know some people are saying that the Bible is the exact book written by God Himself and man has not edited, tainted and or manipulated it at all. I will just shake my head, whatever. That will be explored later in this book.

Throughout world history so called Christian nations gained respect among other nations by preserving and waving the flag of

Christianity. They were also the dominant military force. Those nations were perceived as countries whose basic existence was built on the foundations of Christianity and the premise that God has anointed them to power because of their professing and acknowledgement of Jesus Christ. Have those nations developed and lived based on Christian principles? Have those nations gained respect of the world by putting their fellow man first, loving their neighbor, and loving their enemies as well?

During the history of Western civilization, monarchies, kingdoms, and countries have risen, fell, and risen again. Wars have been fought in the name of good and evil, in the name of God, in the name of righteousness, and in the name of Jesus Christ. America has claimed to the world that they are the one nation that has risen and endured because of their and religious beliefs. Notice I did not say spiritual beliefs. History books spout the notion that the first settlers came to America because of their religious beliefs and our founding fathers were men of God and believed in Christian principles. If this is true our nation is truly blessed and if it is not, what will become of this great nation. We will discuss this further, later. Will history prove that America has sustained her strength because of God's grace and favor. Or will history trace that America has sustained her strength because of "worldly" attributes. Capitalism and military might. If anyone claims America's capitalistic success can be attributed to any anointing or favor with God, they are an idiot. By the way, my publisher suggested I remove that previous statement. But, instead I will repeat it. If anyone thinks America's economic or military might has anything to do with God's blessing, they are an idiot. Will history reveal that America did not honor what she preached and therefore when it is all said and done lost the favor that was their claim to fame. Like that of Israel of Biblical days. If there was a Jesus Christ who was the Son of God, is he proud of his namesake, and will he lift them up to be the nation that is worthy of His name. There are two main factors in intelligently analyzing and answering these questions. One, what exactly are Christian principles and what are the origins of these principles? Two, has America lived up to those principles? What makes this hard to answer is the fact that people have made the very objective principles and teachings of Jesus, subjective and debatable. More specifically throughout history religious scholars and nations have manipulated the scripture to justify their actions, when their actions should justify the scriptures. But, as I previously stated, some of you don't believe that fact. And make no mistake, all religions, and all dominating nations have used religion to further their political, social and economic causes. Many have used religion to further their colonialist views, and fought wars based on these views. Has the United Sates ever justified war, murder, oppression, colonialism, slavery, preemption or nuclear proliferation based on their take that it was justified or honored by God. Of course not! Remember Christianity is about knowing God's compassion, humanity and brotherly love. As is also Islam and every other religion in its purest form. Make no mistake about it, every religion in its purest form is about the acknowledgement, worship and obedience to one Supreme Being. The same Supreme Being, because there is only one, though religions have named them. That actually could be another book. Throughout history Christians have claimed to be the true believers of this concept of "love thy neighbor". And for what is it worth nations world-wide have looked to this great nation to practice what it preaches and to be an example. I think we have had moments in our history were we stood up for justice, truth, morality and brotherly love. But those moments have been far and between too few.

So back to the question. Is America a true Christian nature, according to the scriptures? Not according to opinions given by those who think their race or social status is superior. Has any nation been a true Christian nation? And if not why?

Before we get into answering this, let us take a look at spiritual Biblical messages and principles have been taught and handed down throughout time. Then we will look at how the teachings of Jesus Christ followed these principles based on what the scriptures taught and interpreted as the wishes and will of the Supreme

Being (God). We will also have to discuss how the teachings of Jesus were interpreted throughout the years, changed throughout generations and forgotten through most of history.

Prior to the New Testament, Gods' children either believed or did not believe. There were not hundreds of interpretations of who the Supreme Being was, exclusive of idols. Those who believed in one Supreme Being were His followers or His children and those who did not believe in a single Supreme Being were just considered pagans or idol worshippers. As a matter of fact all major subsequent religions professed the Oneness of God no matter what they called Him. Moses, all the great Kings, the lands, and a majority of the conquest were all similarly mentioned in all religious doctrines prior to the confusion and addition of the New Testament. All the major religions even prophesized about the coming of the Messiah, the Savior, or the prophet who would reveal the truth of man. What differs is who that Messiah was. And just in case no one knows, the two religions who claim to follow the true Messiah actually agree one hundred and ten percent on the message the Messiah taught… though the origins of that person or Being greatly differs. What do you think man has fought over and spent centuries arguing and rationalizing? The message or the origin? Do not be afraid to answer the question. For centuries man fought and argued about the origins of this Messiah and seemed to have put aside the message. So that is what we are going to concentrate on. The message. Why? Because there are constant, repeatable messages throughout the early history of religion. Those constants are universal messages of war, slavery, annihilation and despair. NOT. I just wanted to make sure you were following this. The universal message was and still should be of hope, peace, brotherly love, mercy and compassion. But something happened throughout history. The message was diluted, misguided, and twisted to justify the hypocrisy of man's search for wealth, treasures, land, power and self-righteousness. And just how the religious opinions, rituals and contradictions of today's religions have turned many away, so did they throughout history. You see we go through seasons, cycles, phases in history were the essence of who we are as humans and as spiritual beings are tested. Though many may not want to accept this, we even go through religious wars, which result in spiritual awakenings. And the essence of who we are, is based on our hearts, and our commitment to serving that one God, regardless of what we call Him, just as we were told throughout the Scriptures of all major religions. For those who do not believe in God, the point stays the same. Some have love in their hearts and some do not. The essence of who God wants us to be is also in the scriptures and was repeatedly told to us by prophets, disciples, apostles, and for all those who believe Jesus, Mohammed and God Himself. Christians are waiting for the second coming of Christ, Jews are waiting for their Messiah, Hindus are waiting for their next Avatar, Zoroastrian are waiting for coming of Shah Bahram, and Buddhist are waiting for the coming of fifth Buddha. Does anyone know who Muslims and the Qu'ran says will one come back at the end of days? Look it up. Different religions call him by different names but they all refer to the same thing. Again, what are we debating the message or the origin?

Since the point of this book is to analyze our great nation to determine the validity of its Christian stature and to determine whether or not Jesus would be proud, we will only look at things He taught, His Father taught and the lessons His disciples passed on. Jesus knew that another cycle was coming. He knew that the injustices of man were leading them down a dark road, irrecoverable and destructive. He knew our practice of worship, rituals, and precepts did nothing to help our understanding, and love of God. He knew that God was not pleased with the mumbo jumbo, and the self righteousness of those claiming to be all spiritual. He knew that man had once again lost their way and turned their backs on the poor, hungry, and weak. He knew that man had once again reverted to the philosophy of "Self ", and He knew man needed to be saved…. from themselves.

Okay, we are going to revisit this thought. But let us look at what basic principles Jesus wanted us to adopt, and where did those principles originate from. And as previously mentioned we are going to use the Bible. Why? Because we are talking about Christianity. Do not feel left out followers of Islam, your turn is going to come up. As we look at the Biblical principles of Jesus and teachings of the Bible, I will try to stay away from subjective stories and beliefs. Why? Because as previously mentioned we need to focus on the message and not the particulars and inconsequential things which people dispute but have no relevance to our understanding of who we should be as children of God. We may touch on a few points which may help to prove that many have never really read the Bible but just memorized the stories. And we may touch on a few points to prove that many may have read the stories, but never comprehended them. You see, just as a child we learn reading comprehension, to help us be able to read, retain, analyze and draw conclusions. But for some reason when it comes to the most important thing in our lives as possibly determining our salvation, we do not really comprehend anything, but blindly accept someone else's interpretation and analytical view of what was written. If you do something because you say it is in the Bible, but do not know where it is or what the scripture says about it, you must admit you do so not because it is in the Bible, but because someone may have told you it was in the Bible. Now as I stated some of these things do not impact our relationship with God, but do impeded our ability to understand major truths about those we call religious scholars. And it is those people and religious institutions that we have honored and devoted our trust to throughout history that have been responsible for distorting clear and irrefutable truths in the Bible and other old text scripture.

So what are those irrefutable truths? Those who sacrifice, show unconditional love and put others first, are rewarded, exalted and given favor. Those who are selfish and lead people astray were condemned. That is what every religious text teaches. Let us look at the Bible.

The Bible is the foundation of Christianity, and Jesus taught that the scriptures were the foundation. It holds the teachings and expectations for Christians. It is supposedly His written word through his servants for his people. The Bible consists of 39 books from the Old Testament and 27 book from the New Testament. The Old Testament describes the old covenant God made with Israel while the New Testament is about the new covenant through Jesus Christ and God's people. The entire book includes personal stories, poetic works, prophetic stories, God's laws for his people, and apocalyptic works. The central figure in Christianity is Jesus Christ. As the Son of God, he came to earth to teach about love and fellowship. He represents the person that all Christians must strive to be. Important point, so take note. Christians believe that he is the only one that ever lived on earth that can be called perfect from all worldly sins. Another important thing to understand is that most Christians believe Jesus was God. That will play a major role in the development of the Christians religion during Western civilization. Jesus was here on earth to teach of God's plan for all of humanity and to save the people of the world from their transgressions.

In Christianity as in all major religions, God is almighty and rules over all of heaven and earth. He is the one that created the earth and one day will cast judgment over the entire earth. Christians put their faith that through Jesus Christ, people can be saved from this judgment. By believing that Jesus Christ is Lord and Savior, the Spirit of God was crucified and rose from the dead to save us from our sins, a person can be saved. This belief has encouraged many and falsely emboldened others.

With an approximately 1.7 billion people worldwide, Christianity is arguably the largest religion in the world today. Starting after His death Christianity is based on the teachings and life of Jesus Christ. Some say Christianity was founded in the first century in Palestine by the disciples of Jesus. Other say it wasn't actually founded until the 4th century. Many missionaries spread it, despite heavy persecution, throughout the Roman Empire. Perhaps the most notable missionary was Paul. The various books written by Jesus' followers after his death, called the New Testament, along with the Old Testament makes up the Christian Bible. The Bible holds all the teachings of Jesus on how all Christians should live out their lives. For the purpose of understanding the history of this great country it isn't important whether you believe all this. What matters is that one understands that our leaders claim they believe it. It does not even matter at this point if you believe in Jesus. Why? Because as we explore his teachings we will find out that everything he said was based on simple spiritual principles in the Old Testament, and throughout all religious doctrines prior to his birth. So we will know what the principles of Christianity are way before we even get to facts and fictions about Jesus.

Let me reword this to make sure everyone comprehends the point I am attempting to get across. Through sermons, parables, lessons and walk, Jesus told everyone man has lost their way. And he taught everyone to believe in God as they did back in the "old days". To love God and show this love by the way they treat others. It wasn't rocket science. Do the right thing. The message, throughout time. Jesus wanted us to follow the message God gave His people throughout time, and from the beginning What message did God give to His people to follow? And by the way His people were actually ALL people not just one group. That will become evident later. When we read and comprehend the stories of the Old Testament we see a reoccurring theme or message. Every principal, every character, and every Biblical hero earned favor with God because of something they did. Some act of loyalty, act of kindness and/or compassion and some display of wisdom. And every person mentioned in the Old Testament who lost favor and was destroyed by God (if you believe He kills those who misbehave) was so because of something they did. Some act of unkindness, disrespect, or disloyalty.

We will look at these Biblical heroes to see what constants prevail throughout. What principles are taught throughout each of the thirty nine books of the Old Testament. For some I will preaching to the choir, because I know all the Christians reading this know all of this already. And do not worry I am not going to waste time debating whether God created the heavens, earth, animals, and humans all in literally seven days. If you believe that, power to you.

We will correlate all the principles, parables and stories of obedience, loyalty and humanity to the teachings presented by Jesus. Whose life or story in the Bible should we examine? It really does not matter, for the lessons and outcomes are all the same. When debating the Bible there are two theological points of view. One the Bible is the authoritative, unadulterated Word of God. Nothing added, nothing missing. And the second point of view is that the Bible only mentions things we need to know, ultimately leaving omitting many stories and fact. I said two theological points of view. There is a third point of view, that the Bible is complete fiction. We will not be tackling that view.

Let us take a brief look at the books of the Old Testament. What are the guiding principles and lessons to be learned in each book? Even though I will summarize all the books of the Bible, I promise not to be too lengthy. It could result in a War and Peace amount of pages.

Chapter One

Old Testament

The Bible begins with the Old Testament which was written over many centuries and many different authors. Since this book is focusing on Christianity I will explain how the Old Testament is divided accordingly. We must understand the Old Testament is agreed upon by many other religions. It is a foundation for which Christian's learned about the Supreme Being they call God. The first five books are the Pentateuch. They consist of Genesis, Exodus, Leviticus, book of Numbers and Deuteronomy. These books were purportedly written by Moses. The second group are historical and tell the history of the Israelites, from their conquest of Canaan to their defeat and exile in Babylon. The books of this group are Joshua, Judges, Ruth, First and Second Samuel, First and Second Kings, First and Second Chronicles, Ezra, Nehemiah and Esther. The third group is called the poetic or the Books of Wisdom. These books are comprised of poems, prayers and words of wisdom dealing, with questions of good and evil in the world. Job, Psalms, Proverbs, Ecclesiastes and Song of Solomon are the books in the third group. The final and fourth group are the books of the biblical prophets. This group is divided into the Major and Minor prophets. Isaiah, Jeremiah, Lamentations, Ezekiel, and Daniel are the major prophets, while Hosea, Joel, Amos, Obadiah, Jonah, Micah, Nahum, Habakkuk, Zephaniah, Haggai, Zechariah, and Malachi are the minor prophets. These books highlight men and woman chosen by God and give clear examples of the consequences of turning away from God. Last tidbit. The Protestant Bible is comprised of 39 books. The Catholic, Eastern Orthodox and Oriental Orthodox comprise up to 49 books. Now let's get the show on the road.

Genesis is the first book of the Bible and tells the story of the creation of the universe and man. It is also the first book that reveals flaws in popular Christian belief. However I will not go into much detail about that because too many of you may get pissed and stop reading too soon. Genesis begins to make the reader aware of the creation of man and the consequences of doing evil, and being disobedient.

After the creation of man, we read about Adam and Eve. This will be discussed later. The second most important point is the covenant with Noah, the first covenant with all mankind. It is in this very first book that God asks all humanity to construct societies based on the rule of law, the justice and the non-negotiable dignity of human life. Another person equal in importance is Abraham. Nearly three-fourths of Genesis focuses on one particular family, Abraham, and his descendants. One note to make is the fact that the Bible is actually the genealogy of this family traced from Adam to Noah to Joseph in the New Testament. And this brings us back to something I mentioned earlier for those who think Adam was the first man. The bible is the story of the family which were the ancestors of Jesus. Many other humans existed before or during the life of Adam and Eve. Now I am going to hold true to my word and be objective and only use the Bible as my source of reference. Is it of major importance that you believe Adam was the first man? No. But it is important that you understand why the Bible was written. And this is the first step. You have to understand little things like the use of the word "begotten". To understand, further read about the creation in the book of Genesis. Now I know everyone is saying, "I read it a thousand times, and know the story". Well, maybe you have read the Bible a thousand times, but you have not fully comprehended it, if you believe Adam and Eve were the only humans who walked the earth. Let us take a quick look.

In the very first chapter of Genesis Moses tell the story of creation. In six days God created everything. The first two days God created the Earth, with the land and the seas. On the third day after the earth brought forth grass and herb yielding fruit whose seed was in itself God also created the stars (sun) to distinguish the seasons. On the fourth and fifth day God created animals, fish and birds. Whales and cattle are specifically mentioned. Dinosaurs are not mentioned, even though it does say other "creeping things and beast". I guess the cattle lived during the same period as the dinosaurs. Now here we go. On the sixth day God said, ""Let us make man in our image, after our likeness. And let them have dominion over the fish of the sea and over the birds of the heavens and over the livestock and over all the earth and over every creeping thing that creeps on the earth.". Genesis 1:26 (ESV). So God created man in his own image; in the image of God he created them; male and female. So here we have it, God created man in his own image. Clearly and distinctly. Now here is what many have not comprehended. The man and woman he created and told to be fruitful and multiply were not just Adam and Eve. Adam and Eve were the ancestors of Jesus. Why on earth would I say such a thing? One reason, is because I do indeed love God and two, it says so in the scriptures.

We know in Chapter 1 God created man in his own image. But if you read ahead to chapter 2 we find out that God caused it to rain so the seeds would grow and then realized He had no one to till the ground. Were the other humans not wise enough, not trust worthy enough? They were created in His image, according to the scriptures. Anyway, in Genesis 2:6 God creates Adam. Now some may stubbornly argue that the beginning of the second chapter is just recapping the fourth, fifth and sixth day and Adam was that Man created in Chapter 1. Well that is not what Moses said! If you read on, we are told about Adam and Eves son's Cain and Abel. Well we all know the story. Cain was jealous and killed Abel. For doing this horrendous act God banished Cain from his land and sent him out "as a fugitive and a vagabond. Now Cain thought this was unusual and cruel punishment saying, "My punishment is greater than I can bear… I shall be a fugitive… and it shall come to pass that every one that findeth me shall slay me". Genesis 4:14, (NIV) Why did he say everyone? Did God ask him, "What are you talking about, you, Adam and Eve are the only ones on Earth". No He did not. God responded in acknowledgment that there were on fact others, many others, saying, "Whosoever slays Cain, vengeance shall be taken on him seven fold". God substantiated Cain's concern that others may kill him. And when Cain was banished he went to another land, fully populated with people, where he got married. Cain did not marry Eve. He married a fully grown woman whom lived in another fully populated region.

This brings me to another story in Genesis about the Tower of Babel. The people of Babylonia wanted to build a huge tower to tout their greatness. God was disappointed in their disrespect and destroyed the tower but also changed the language of the workers so they could no longer understand one another. The people were dispersed over the face of the earth and this is how all the languages supposedly originated. It clearly says "over the face of the earth". Not a region or continent.

What is my point? The bible is the story of the lineage of Abraham through Jesus (step-father) Joseph. It is not the complete story of mankind!! There were clearly already men and civilization during the time of Adam and Eve. This is reiterated throughout the bible and this book, for those who actually read it! Even Chapter five clarifies saying "This is the book of the generations of Adam". Why is this tidbit important? Because you need to understand the importance, the relevance, the privilege and responsibility one has who claims to be a descendant of Adam, Abraham, Moses, David and Jesus. In short, the Israelites. As we read we will see that throughout history, many did not live up to that obligation. Those generations follow Cain's offspring whom were the "other" humans created in God's image. Those generations were the one's blessed with the covenant. This is being pointed out not to question one's belief, but to set the stage for how religion became to be what it is today.

The main characters of Genesis are Adam, Eve, Cain, Abel, Noah, Abraham, Isaac, Jacob, Joseph and of course the introduction of the devil. Abraham is of course major, since it is his lineage that is the basis for Jesus in the first place. According to the Hebrew Bible, God commands Abraham to offer his son Isaac as a sacrifice. After Isaac is bound to an altar, a messenger from God stops Abraham before He recognized Abraham's faithfulness and in today's term loyalty. But He also told him, it was a test, and that sacrifice is not needed. For he is the one that God chose to give or bless with a covenant. The covenant was a promise not necessarily with Abraham but to his generations to come. Quick note, there are many stories in the Old Testament which tell of various test and disciplinary actions God placed on the humans He created in His own image. Joseph has an important role considering the two perspectives or schools of teaching. You can focus on how God blessed Joseph who was enslaved. Or, you can focus on how the brothers who enslaved Joseph was shown mercy. Throughout the history of slavery and conquest the latter was what was taught and repeatedly drilled in the hearts of those enslaved or tamed.

The second book of the Old Testament is Exodus. This book is an account of the increase and growth of the Israelites in Egypt. It outlines the oppression of Abraham's offspring and preparations for departure out of Egypt and their journey from Egypt to Sinai. Exodus also contains the first account of any type of "law" and the establishment of the institutions by which the organization of the people was completed, and the existence of theocracy. We learn that during this time, kingdom of priests and the first holy nation were introduced. Exodus makes reader aware that if you confess that you believe in Him, it better show by your actions. It is also in the second book of the Bible that we lose the understanding of our purpose. This is one of the overarching principles, we will later discuss. The main point to highlight is God's disapproval of slavery. Many Christians for some reason use the Bible as an excuse or justification for slavery. But they should pay more attention to how He freed those enslaved and the wrath brought upon the oppressors. Slavery was the result of man having free will, eating the apple and not appreciating God. Not the cursed minds of generations of wick nations. They were the ones enslaving others. The second major point was of course the Ten Commandments. Main character Moses went into the mountains and came down with the stone tablets. The Ten Commandments. And you can just go through them and tell yourself how many we follow, and how many we break bases on political, social, judicial and theological reasons. For further knowledge, the Ten Commandments were only the first written and "recorded" account of laws or rules to live by. God expected His people to obey, after all He freed them and protected them. I am not going to go into the Ten Commandments. I will assume everyone is familiar with them.

Leviticus, the third book, contains a series of laws regarding sacrifices and various types of offerings. It also introduces the duties and obligations of "priest". This book as previously mentioned, was written by Moses though in a style where it seemed that God is actually the main orator. He outlines laws the people of Israel should adhere to pertaining to purity and obedience, and lays down warnings for disobedience to His commandments. Israel was intended to represent God's kingdom. God established a king to sort of manage all aspects of Israel's life. One important duty of the Israelites was to offer sacrifices to God. And though they may resemble other Old Testament sacrifices the type and significance of them were specific to the types of atonement given. The reason they were willing to make sacrifices was because they knew they had to. They knew they had screwed up. The days or moments of atonement were to redeem one for different sins, purifying a particular place or ensuring good health. For each sin or atonement, there were different offering required. And, no, not a tithe to be used for the benefit or gain of the pastor. These principles for living are also in the New Testament. Do you know where? Hebrews. The main point are the laws set, which mainly deal with the obvious and yet forgotten laws. Do not do anything to endanger you neighbor, do not pervert justice, do not show partiality to the poor, or favoritism to the rich and ultimately - Love thy neighbor as thyself. Wow, ok did you read that? The main characters are Moses and Aaron.

The next book, Numbers is so called, because it contains the first record or census of the Israelites, and is sometimes called the Book of Moses. This book gives us details as to the route of the Israelites in the wilderness and their principal encampments. It also contains further laws for them to follow and practical insights for daily living. By practical, I mean obvious. Numbers also re-introduces slavery and the plight of the Israelites. Their slavery is a direct result of their continuous selfishness and jealousy, in the wake of all their blessings. The book specifically points out, that the disobedient generation all died in the wilderness. We see in this history, on the one hand, the unceasing care of the Almighty over his people, and yet, the murmurings and rebellions by which disobedient Israelites offended their heavenly Protector, and incurred His displeasure, provoking him to say that they should "not enter into his rest" because of their unbelief. One of the main points, is God telling those he looked out for…"do not forget what I've done for you… and do not think it was your own power that freed you" Main characters Moses and Aaron.

Deuteronomy consists chiefly of three parts, spoken to all Israelites in the plains of Moab, in the eleventh month of the last year of their wanderings. The first part summarizes the chief events of the last forty years in the wilderness. This includes reminders of the command to be obedient to the divine ordinances, and warnings against the danger of forsaking the God of their fathers. The second part contains a recapitulation of the law already given by God at Mount Sinai, together with many authoritative counsel and warnings. This includes how they should behave and the rules they were to follow when they settled in Canaan. Do you remember Canaan? Do you think they followed any rules or were obedient? The last part relates to the sanctions of the law, the blessings to the obedient, and the curse that would fall on the rebellious. Moses ask them to adhere faithfully to the covenant God had made with them, and so secure for themselves and their posterity the promised blessings. The main point summarized is Moses telling the people, "do not get cocky and arrogant, remember what you went through" God looked out for you, so do not turn around and ask, "what has He done for us lately". Many woman should heed to this when asking their man that very question! Just joking, don't get mad!

Can you tie this to anything else that happened in our history?

You have to also remember, that because of Moses disobedience God did not allow His main dude at the time, Moses, to enter the land in which he spent his life leading his people to. You may or may not believe this. But Christians, Catholics and Protestant, as well as those who adopted Judaism do. If God chastised Moses, what chance do you think you would of had? We will get back to later. "Follow justice and justice alone, so that you may live and possess the land the LORD your God is giving you" Deuteronomy 16:20 (NIV). I would conclude that if we do not follow justice then the land God has given us will be zapped under our feet.

The book of the Bible Joshua contains a history of the Israelites from the death of Moses to that of Joshua whom took over after Moses death. It is basically the story of Israel from the conquest of Canaan to the Babylonian exile. The conquest of their land and they become slaves, once again. The book points out, again, that the Israelites did not follow God's instructions. The book also points out God's mercy, His approval and commandment for the annihilation of the Canaanites. And the third rise of Israel. This causes great confusion amongst those who argue that either God isn't as merciful as we say, He does not exist or He is just plain evil. After all, He did not forgive the Canaanites. For all the Christians who believe the story, there are two rules of thought. One group justifies the practice genocide and destroying of a nation of people for they believe God will understand. The Christian view states, "that is why Jesus came in the first place, to stop kingdoms and nations from doing things like this. Also, so people would stop atrocities in God's name or just insane people saying God spoke to them told them and it was the right thing to do. Quick note, if this account is true we must not get it twisted and we must remember. According to the scripture God destroyed the Canaanites because they were all evil. The entire nation. Not just a few idiot leaders. And we will see, when it was time for God's discipline, he usually fulfilled prophecy that effected an entire nation.

The entire book of Judges covers the time period from Joshua to the birth of Samuel. It gives accounts of how the Israelites repeatedly screwed up, committing unconscionable acts and the ultimate consequences. The stories follow the same old stories. The Israelites are unfaithful to God and their enemies take over. It is called Judges because God attempted to have "rulers", to keep the peace. The book tells of twelve judges, each with a different degree of importance and success. All told God's selections failed miserably.

Ruth is short book that tells a simple story. But it is clearly intends to give examples of faith, patience, industry, and kindness, as well as, indications of the care which God takes of those who put their trust in him. It gives an account of a woman named Naomi going to Moab with her husband Elimelech and of her subsequent return to Bethlehem. Naomi had two sons Mahlon and Chilion. Mahlon married Ruth. So the story tells of Naomi's return to Bethlehem with her daughter-in-law Ruth after the death of her two sons Mahlon and Chilion. The book discusses the subsequent marriage of Boaz and Ruth who was not born a Jew. But she was allegiant to her Jewish family. She was sort of Jewish by choice. The book of Ruth highlights the birth of Obed. Why is Obed's birth important? Because it was ultimately the lineage of David.

Samuel written in two books comprises a period of about a hundred years, and explains God's law for Israel under the guidance of the prophets. In short, Hannah, one of Elkanah's wives was unable to bear a child. So he went to a priest and prayed to a priest Eli for favor with God. Hannah then gave birth to Samuel. Samuel became a prophet and named Saul as King. Now that is where the book gets convoluted. God anoints Samuel to serve as a prophet and judge. But after many years of peace Israel went to it is old ways. And when Samuel became old Israel's enemies attack. Now this was an important time spiritually and politically. Israel was transformed into a monarchy where Samuel appointed a man name Saul king. Saul happened to be a self-centered, approval needing Trumpish type guy. He not only disrespected God's will but he endangered the people of Israel by having them turn against God as well. So, Saul was out and David would become king. If we all remember David was the one who slayed Goliath. Saul feared that David would one day seize his kingdom, and spends the rest of his life hunting David down. But faithful David would become king. A verse in 1 Samuel 12:23-25 (NIV) reads, "But be sure to fear the Lord and serve him faithfully with all your heart; consider what great things he has done for you. Yet if you persist in doing evil, both you and your king will perish."

The second book of Samuel contains a history of the reign of David over Judah. David was a good king who served the Lord and cared for his people, until he wasn't. David snatched Bathsheba from her husband. As punishment the child David conceived with Bathsheba dies. Key events of David's reign were his bringing the Ark of the Covenant to Jerusalem, his founding of an eternal royal dynasty, and his preparations for the construction of the Temple. What are key points and principles of obedience? David's indiscretion with Bathsheba.

Something else I would like to point out is a passage in 1 Samuel 10:6 (ISV)) which states "The Spirit of the Lord will come upon you in power and you will prophesy with them, and you will be changed into a different person. Once these signs are fulfilled do whatever your hands finds to do, for God is with you". Why do I point this out? Very important to understand. Two parts here. The Holy Spirit coming upon oneself, that person prophesizing and three you having the power to do all things. We will discuss it later when we explore the New Testament and the ideologies of evangelical ministries. Remember, being filled with the Holy Spirit.

The Book of Kings continues the accounts during the reign of chosen leaders mainly Solomon It highlights the division of the united Israel into the southern kingdom of Israel and the northern kingdom of Judah. This time God pays disloyalty with immediate punishment, the faithlessness of kings was punished on later generations. The sins of the father sort of thing.

Chronicles is another book divided into two separate books. Much of the content of Chronicles is a repetition of material from other books of the Bible, from Genesis to Kings. It tells more about lineage of David, Solomon and The kingdom of Judah. These two books detail several important implications for our lives. The first is that no matter how bad things get remember how God has helped us. The second is God is not pleased with half-hearted fake apathetic love for Him. If you love Him, He says do it with all your heart. Do not just talk the talk. Walk the walk.

Ezra is the record of events occurring at the close of the Babylonian exile. The king of Persia was ordained to commission a Jewish leader. There were three leaders picked. The tasks of the three leaders were first restore the temple (Zerubbabel), then the community of Israel (Ezra), and finally the build the walls separating the Temple from the outside world (Nehemiah). And of course this book is during the reign of Ezra whom struggled to purify the Jews from marriage with non-Jews. There are two main stories. The story outlines the history of the first return of those who had been exiled. The second part of the book is the history of the second return under Ezra.

The book Nehemiah which may historically be regarded as a continuation of the book of Ezra, consists of four parts. First, an account of the rebuilding of the wall of Jerusalem, and of the register Nehemiah had found of those who had returned from Babylon. Second an account of the state of religion among the

Jews during this time. Third, the increase of the inhabitants of Jerusalem, the census of the adult male population, and names of the chiefs, together with lists of priests and Levites. The fourth part was the dedication of the wall of Jerusalem, the arrangement of the temple officers, and the reforms carried out by Nehemiah. Many scholars say this book closes the actual history of the Old Testament. From here on throughout the Bible we are further introduced to the other nations. Persia, Jordan, Arabia. Remember that though God scattered people all over the world, the nations we are introduced to are still in the same geographical area.

The book Esther is named for the "star" of the story, a young Jewish girl named Hadassah who was taken from her guardian, Mordecai, and forced to compete for the affection of the king. This unlikely contestant of a beauty pageant was crowned queen of Persia and renamed Esther, meaning "star." The events in the book of Esther occurred from 483 BC to 473 BC, during the first half of the reign of King Xerxes (the movie "300"), who chose Esther as his queen. During this time period, the first remnant of Jews who had returned to Judah were struggling to reestablish temple worship according to the Law of Moses. Esther and Mordecai were Jewish but decided not to go back to Judah, along with many other Jews and stayed in Susa, the capital city of Persia, in which the story is set.

Why is Esther so important? There are scholarly reasons, laymen's reasons and my reasons. Esther is the only book in the Bible not to mention the name of God, but His presence is felt throughout the story. Esther was a Jewish slave who became queen and her story speaks to Hebrew and those of Jewish faith. Life can be hard, difficult times happen, and pain cannot be avoided. But the book of Esther encourage you that God is always present. Trust and obey, as Esther did. And watch God silently weave all events for His glory and for our good. Mordecai says to Esther as she's considering whether she should advocate for her people: "And who knows but that you have come to your royal position for such a time as this" One of my many best verses, "For Such a Time as This"

This story about Job is very meaningful, parabolic, and mind grabbing, but for me kind of unbelievable. The meat of the story is that God is chilling out with Satan and bragging on His faithful and loyal servant Job. Satan request that God test Job by having him suffer. Really, really suffer. Job lost his wife, children, his wealth and his health. If you believe that God would destroy the life of a spiritual, faithful obedient person to prove a point to the devil, then again power to you. The story points out that one's love for God should not be directly related to ones suffering or wealth, Jobs exaltation to God when he was at his poorest and weakest proved his unwavering love. Okay point taken. I personally do not believe God would do that to prove something to the devil.

Psalms is a collection of lyrical poems, it is sort of a time out for praise. Psalms is comprised of ancient hymnals and the emotion of God's people. Psalms of lament express the author's crying out to God in difficult circumstances. There are Psalms of praise and worship, also called hymns, wisdom psalms, royal psalms, victory psalms, Law psalms, and songs of Zion. The Book of Psalms is divided into five sections. The first section emphasize how God is beside us. The second tells us how God goes before us. The third book of Psalms reminds us that God is all around us and the fourth focuses on how God is above us. In the fifth and final section, the spotlight is on how the God is among us. The Book is geared at reminding the Israelites who God is, His eternal presence. And His watchful eye. I am sure if you know nothing about Psalms you have heard this. "The Lord is my shepherd; I shall not want. He makes me lie down in green pastures. He leads me beside still waters. Psalms 23 (KJV). And so forth.

The book of Proverbs is a collection of moral and philosophical compositions of a wide range of subjects presented in a poetic form. It reminds us how the Bible recommends common sense and discretion. It drills in us the value of intelligence, prudence and of a good education. The whole book is bases on these truths. It talks some much of the intangible honorable and good characteristics of human nature that most overlook throughout the Bible.

"Open your mouth for the mute, for the rights of all who are destitute. Open your mouth, judge righteously, defend the rights of the poor and needy." Proverbs 31:8-9 (ESV)

Ecclesiastes is a book many people miss all together. It identifies a man who had sinned in giving way to selfishness and sensuality. To most readers the author seems to have given up on all previous Proverbs. He later pays the penalty of that sin in the weariness and despair of life. He soon learns the lessons which God meant to teach him. The writer concludes by pointing out that the secret of a true life is that a man should use the vigor of his youth serving God. The key message is all man's efforts to find happiness apart from God are without result. A verse in the last chapter reads "Now all has been heard; here is the conclusion of the matter: Fear God and keep his commandments, for this is the whole duty of man. For God will bring every deed into judgment, including every hidden thing, whether it is good or evil."

The Song of Solomon is simply a romantic love poem describing the love of a young Solomon and a Shulamite maiden who became his first bride. I bet you didn't know that!

The next section of the Old Testament are the Prophets. Prophets were regarded as direct spokesmen for God. In Christianity the figures widely recognized as prophets are those mentioned as such in the Old Testament and the New Testament. It is believed that prophets are chosen and called by God. They were seen to speak the words of God to the people of Israel. Their main role was to predict future events, and to call upon the public to repent and return to the true faith. The term "major" in this context means that the prophet's message was preserved in a lengthy book and covered a wider variety of subjects than did the minor prophets. There were of course dozens or perhaps hundreds of prophets whose stories were never recorded.

The book of Isaiah consists of the reigns of many Kings and many prophecies. They tell of the reign of Uzziah of Hezekiah and the reign of Isaiah. Isaiah's ministry extended over a period of sixty-four years. The book, as a whole, has been divided into three main parts. The first thirty- five chapters is almost wholly prophetic. The book tells of Israel's enemy Assyria and presents the Messiah as a mighty Ruler and King. Four chapters are historical, relating to the times of Hezekiah. The third is prophetical, Israel's enemy Babylon, describing the Messiah as a suffering victim, meek and lowly. The most important prophesy for Christians, Isaiah reveals the coming of an anointed one, a prophet, the Messiah or as Christians believe… Jesus Christ. The Messiah would be the ultimate advocate and cheerleader for God's desire to have man seek justice and humanity. Verse 1:17 of Isaiah (ESV) states, "Learn to do good; seek justice, correct oppression; bring justice to the fatherless, and please the widow's cause," Bring justice to the fatherless, that was definitely prophetic! But not yet realized. The last thing I will mention is the introduction of the "Gifts of the Holy Spirit". Not to be confused with the "Fruits of the Holy Spirit"

Jeremiah was a priest called the "weeping prophet" because of his prophesies or predictions of the fate of Jerusalem, the Southern Kingdom of Judah and other nations. His recorded ministry is from 626 to 586 BCE. Jeremiah warned the people not to use idols and he highlights of the sins of the Jews. Jeremiah described the one God of Jacob as the Maker or Creator, whose name is "The Lord Almighty". Jeremiah is concerned about why wicked men seem prosperous. This was a still is a common theme amongst spiritual people. Jeremiah warned against "false prophets" that do not speak for God. As Isaiah did, Jeremiah warned of the future around his time (or even possibly yet to come now) of the "last days". Jeremiah believed that everyone is rewarded according to his life and deeds not his father's life and deeds. Jeremiah warned of God's tremendous displeasure with people worshipping other "gods" and material things.

Two sections in the book tells the hopes of better times. The principal Messianic prophecies are a compilation of over one hundred in the Old Testament regarding the Messiah or Jesus Christ. A word came to Jeremiah from the Lord telling him to take his place and shout God's message. He told his people that the Lord Almighty says' Reform your ways and your actions, and I will let you live in this place" Jeremiah 7;3 (NIV). God's message also includes that one should not trust in deceptive words, they should not oppress the foreigner, the fatherless or the widow. God also states that one should not shed innocent blood. He also warns against those who may steal, murder, commit adultery and perjury, and then basically go to church and claim to be God's child. He adds that if you do those things you and your offspring will be cast out of His house and banished. Remember, do not oppress the foreigner. Jeremiah's also points out that false religion is worthless and false teachers are in trouble.

The Book of Lamentations begins with sufferings and just dues of the sinful people of Israel. It describes the horrible invasion of the city, the way its inhabitants turned to cannibalism due to starvation. Like all books of the Bible, it traces it only to the people's sins. In my opinion foretells of the continual discretions and sins of not only the Israelites, but of nations to come. Not Muslim, Buddhist or Hindu countries, but Christian ones.

The next book tells the story of Ezekiel. Like other prophets, Ezekiel says that God is very dismayed by worship of idols and "gods" and at "false prophets" and hypocrites. Ezekiel taught that "...a righteous man does what is just and right... and said God will judge, each one according to his ways and his own actions. Something that many Christians do not want to believe. He believed unlike many Christian zealots that one will be judged according to his or her many acts. Ezekiel pointed out the analogies of life and God's promise. He made sure he included the tribes the Southern Kingdom (including Jerusalem and the two tribes of Judah and Benjamin) and the Northern Kingdom (including the other ten tribes, called Israel). However, when the Hebrews were brought back to Jerusalem, Ezekiel felt that all the twelve tribes of Israel would be united with a new Temple in Jerusalem. The key to this point is ALL twelve tribes.

The book of Daniel tell the story how he was captured and enslaved by the Babylonians. Like Esther he had favor and rose to became a member of the royal house of nobility. Daniel survived many disastrous moments and spent the rest of his long life in the city of Babylon, in the service of the royal court. There are two well-known stories from Daniel. The fiery furnace and the lions' den. There are two perspectives. One being David was spared because of his faithfulness to God. The other perspective is that his plotters were killed because of their wickedness.

The next section of Books are the Minor prophets. The list of minor prophets, consists of those individuals who are recorded as having had a visionary or prophetic experience, but without a history of any major or consistent prophetic calling. A final list contains the names of those described in the Bible as prophets, but are presented as either misusing this gift or as fraudulent.

Hosea, a prophet of the Northern Kingdom (Israel), tells about his wife Gomer, who was a prostitute. Hosea sees that Israel has also acted like a prostitute, serving their "gods," Despite this, God still loves the Jews, who will return to the Lord in the "last days".

One should notice there are a lot of righteous men in the Bible marrying or hanging out with prostitutes. And figuratively the repeated claim of Israel and other nations acting like "prostitutes" Remember this very important tidbit. If not a prostitute a woman of ill repute. It will come up again and again.

In the Book of Joel there is great devastation of plague and famine caused by a huge locust plague. The Prophet Joel warned the people of Judah, that the day of the Lord though great, it will be equally dreadful. It is the first Book that gives imagery to the scripture. Joel states that at the time the Lord comes, the "sun will be turned to darkness and the moon to blood...everyone who calls on the Name of the Lord will be saved". This is paraphrased and mentioned in several other books. Like the other prophets Joel stated that, the Day of the Lord or Judgment Day was near.

Now throughout the bible, many lessons and many acts of discipline were given. God punished the accused or guilty, God punished the guilty party's ancestral lineage and now handed down judgement by means of external naturalistic phenomena. So far water and floods, disease and locust destroy mankind. What type of events do you think will spawn judgement day in our times?

Amos, a herdsman, and a prophet from Southern Judah lived during the time of King Jeroboam. This was a time in history where Israel had its greatest time of prosperity, but God would test the Hebrews and scatter Israel across the world because of their immorality, social injustice and the fact that the rich were getting richer at the expense of the poor. Sound familiar? "Therefore this is what the Lord, the LORD God Almighty, says: "There will be wailing in all the streets and cries of anguish in every public square…." Amos 5;18 (NIV)

Obadiah tells of the fall of more nations. An important point to this book is that God wants brotherly love, not only between blood brothers but among all people. Another Book telling of the fall of a nation and simply because love and respect for other nations and peoples were ignored. It's okay, shake your head at the irony.

The next book tells of Jonah who was appointed by God to tell the people of Ninevah of their destruction because of their wickedness. Jonah was afraid of the task set forth by God so he fled and hid on a ship. When a raging storm occurred the sailors realized that Jonah was to blame. Jonah admitted this and was thrown overboard to please God, and was then swallowed by a whale for three days and then was "vomited" up onto dry land. If you believe that power to you. Jonah then delivered the message to the people of Ninevah, they prayed to be saved, and they were saved from destruction. An important fact. God loves and needs all. Gentiles as well as Jews. The main point of this book is that everyone is a child of God; not just the Jews or Israelites. This is also a reoccurring theme throughout the Bible (Old and New Testament)

Micah was another prophet speaking of the last days. Same old song. His primary message dealt with the growing wickedness of Southern Israel. As with the other prophets he told the people that God wants us to live a life of humility, mercy and justice, by conquering lands and enslaving people… of course not. Just checking, to see if you're still with me. His message was that God wants us to rid our lives of idolatry, greed, exploitation and religious hypocrisy. Another point is God will forgive, but he won't wait forever for one to repent without sending out justice.

Micah 6:8 reads something like this, again paraphrased, "He has shown you, what is good. And all God requires is that you act justly, have mercy and to walk humbly with your God"

Nahum portrays the downfall of the Assyria Empire, and its capital city, Nineveh one of Israel's worst oppressors. It is God's way of re-enforcing the fact that he will destroy evil empires. It shows examples of how God works in history in every age. Nahum tells the rulers of Nineveh and the Assyrian empire, that God said, "…I He will prepare their grave…" Nahum says that God is good and knows all who trust Him, and He knows His enemies, who will be destroyed. Do we as Christians know who are our enemies? For a lot of things, we are.

The Book of Habakkuk is the eighth book of the 12 minor prophets of the Bible. The major theme of Habakkuk going from a faith doubt to absolutely trusting in God. The main conflict is Habakkuk questioning why God would let the Babylonians plunder Judah and the Israelites for their sins. Habakkuk sees the pain of his people and openly questions the wisdom of God. God then explains that He will also judge the Chaldeans, and much more harshly for their violence. Basically, by the final chapter, Habakkuk expresses his ultimate faith in God, even if he does not fully understand God's plan.

One of my favorite scriptures from this book is, "The vision is yet for an appointed time. Though it may tarry wait on it. For it shall surely come!" Paraphrasing of course.

The Book of Zephaniah is the ninth of the Twelve Minor Prophets. Zephaniah, of course, focuses on "the day of the Lord," The day of the Lord is simply a day of judgement. In Zephaniah it tells us, "The great day of the LORD is near and coming quickly. Listen! Zephaniah 1:14 (KJV) The cries of even mighty men on the day of the LORD will be bitter" My own words, but means the same as all the Biblical versions. The book begins by describing God's judgement and reinforcing the wrath to come to the Israelites. Zephaniah occasionally mentioned how Judah refuse to obey its covenant obligations with God despite having seen Israel's repeated exile. This was despite the fact that Judah's exile was attributed to God's anger against Israel's disobedience to his covenant. In this historical context, Zephaniah urges Judah to obedience to God, saying that "perhaps" he will forgive them if they do. As common in the Bible, by humbly seeking refuge in God a few survive God's judgement in Zephaniah. The book concludes hope and joy, as God reined joy over His people.

The Book of Haggai is the third-to-last of the Minor Prophets and another book of the Hebrew Bible. It is a short book, consisting of only two chapters. The historical setting dates around 520 BCE before the Temple has been rebuilt. The Book of Haggai is named after its presumed author, the prophet Haggai. There is no biographical information given about the prophet in the Book of Haggai. The book consist of several prophecies.

Haggai's message is filled with an urgency for the people to proceed with the rebuilding of the second Jerusalem temple. Haggai attributes a recent drought to the people's refusal to rebuild the temple. He sees the rebuilding of the temple as a key to Jerusalem's reaffirmation and ultimate glory. I think this is ironic. Haggai wanted to please God. But deep down it was either for selfish gain, being misplaced or being just clueless to all prophecies. The book ends with the prediction of the downfall of kingdoms, with one Zerubbabel, governor of Judah, as the Lord's chosen leader.

Zechariah also a Minor Prophet was the grandson of a priest, and prophesied to the people of Judah after they returned from their seventy years of exile in Babylon. Zechariah along with his grandfather was among the first group of Israelites allowed back. The book begins recalling the nation's history, to give a warning to the new generation. The book is a series of eight visions. The main emphasis is that God is at work and plans to live again with His people in Jerusalem. He will save them from their enemies and cleanse them from sin. Zechariah's spoke for purity in the priesthood and in the temple. He spoke of the need to eliminate the influence of the governor in favor of the high priest. He tells that God seeks a covenant relationship with his people and will be a God of grace, love and forgiveness. He give a strong message of the need for the high priest to come.

Zechariah 7:9 (NIV), "This is what the Lord Almighty said: 'Administer true justice; show mercy and compassion to one another. Do not oppress the widow or the fatherless, the foreigner or the poor. Do not plot evil against each other..''

Zechariah earned status as a Minor Prophet for whatever reason. But after I read his eloquent words I am reminded that he basically abstained from having any power or anointment from God. Instead he deferred to the yet to arrive high priest.

Malachi is the last of the Twelve Minor Prophets making Malachi the last book before the New Testament. The Book of Malachi was written to correct the lax religious and social behavior of the Israelites, He speaks particularly to the priests. Even after the prophets urged the people of Judah and Israel that their exile was punishment for failing to uphold their covenant with God, it was not long after that the people's commitment to God began, once again, to falter. It was in this context that the prophet commonly referred to as Malachi, delivered his prophecy. Malachi has the people of Israel go through a question and answer session to explain their doubt of God's love for them. Malachi accuses those he speaks to of failing to respect God as God deserves. One way is their skimping on the sacrifices offering blind, lame and sick animals for sacrifice because they thought nobody would notice and they thought they were special. Malachi also criticizes the people for questioning God's justice. Malachi also states God is sending a curse on the priests who have not honored him. He goes on to say, the people are not giving God all that God deserves. Just as primarily because the priests have been offering unacceptable sacrifices, The result of these shortcomings is that the people come to believe that no good comes out of serving God. Malachi assures his audience that the differences between those who served God faithfully and those who did not will become clear. If the people of Israel were chastised for skimping on offerings, what do you think Malachi would say about those getting rich on the kindness and severance of others.

Many of the verses in Malachi are repeated throughout the New Testament, So there we have it, the first section of the Bible. It introduces us to God, His creation as well as His chosen people and most important confidants. More importantly, we should learn what God expects and the same punishment handed down if we do not live up to God expectations. When we read about all the events and people, we should be able to understand the important principles which came in the form of blessings or lessons. Okay, let us quickly sum up the Old Testament.

One major principle, if in fact you believe what you have read in the 39 books, is that God loves everyone, every race, from every nation. What is the catch or should I say criteria? One criteria is obviously that you love Him. In the Old Testament that love was tested For some nations their love was apparent through they way they lived and treated others.. All the main characters in the Bible went through a series of trials and tribulations.

Who were the main people of the Old Testament? Yes, there was Abraham, Isaac, Jonah, Job, Noah, Joseph and those in the category of the always loyal and faithful. What test did they have to endure? Really, really rough test. In each story the example and test was life affirming. It would always seem harsh. Then there were those chosen by covenant. Throughout the Old Testament the Israelites not only had favor with God, but by right of a covenant were chosen. Then we had those anointed and born to be rulers and Kings. What happened to them? Last, there were the ones who we would not have thought would be anointed by God. How did they fair in this Book of Books? They actually fared better. Will there be any similarities in the New Testament. If so, will you recognize them? God knows one's heart, and judges and test accordingly. That is why I question the Job story and the bet with the Devil. Anyway, today's Christian seems to sell their faith. Brag about how much the go to church or put Christian books out and praise music on when church members visit. Unfortunately, they will be in one of those previous distinct groups and be tested as well. One more thing they should hope, God thinks enough about them to administer a test.

One thing we must note and ingest, every time God unleashed His wrath for people acting unholy, their bad acts were not being poor, gay, disabled, Mexican, African and immigrant or even a prostitute. His wrath was due to those not believing in His gifts, mercy and blessings as well as their self-exaltation. His wrath was due to unappreciative self-professed lovers of God whom acted self-righteous while cheating, lying and committing inhumane acts. His wrath was against those who disrespected, hurt, killed or enslaved His people. He also punished those He gave favor to and anointed them as leaders of people. God expected those He showed favor to act accordingly and follow His laws and commands, written and unwritten. His wrath was on those who claimed to be His rightful heirs. His wrath was on those He put all His chips on and lost. At some point God realized the masses would not get it. God repeatedly expressed for all to have faith in Him. A faith that must be evident when times are at their worst. Two, we can see that there are repeated talk or prophesying of the "messiah" coming back. Why? Because He had to. Why? Because after thousands of years, no one seemed to get it. I shouldn't say no one… but very few. So few, there needed to be a Jesus. And as we will see, so few that the New Testament ends woefully.

In the Bible you do not have to be Jewish to be a man or woman of God. Melchizedek, Abraham's contemporary, was not a member of the covenantal family, but the Bible calls him "a priest of God Most High." Moses' father-in- law, Jethro, a Midianite, gives Israel its first system of governance. And one of the most courageous heroines of the Exodus is an Egyptian princess who rescues Moses and gives his name. "The righteous of every faith, and of every nation, shall have a share in the world to come." I believe this. I repeat. The righteous of every nation. All persons of all races and ethnic origins were, are and will be accepted and blessed by God.

Well, we know for sure, that in the Old Testament God spoke of doing the right thing. What were those things, exclusive of just loving God? He wanted all to show their love for others. He wanted all mankind to love and treat everyone with respect. Wives, families, friends, neighbors, the poor and even ones enemies. What was another principle? Do not think that the size of your kingdom or the amount of your wealth matter, because as they were given they can be taken away. Honor nothing but God and your fellow man. And do it day in and day out, because once you do not you will reap what you sow. When I mentioned God wanted us to show their love for humanity through his or her actions I also meant we should put God first. One more fact rarely mentioned. God also expressed His desire for us to appreciate value and nurture the earth He entrusted to us. The Old Testament also stresses that it is God, that will judge a nation. It is not within the power of man to judge another man or decide they are better and rule over them. One more important fact revisited. Until the revision of the Old Testament by Shakespeare there was no mention of the word God. Not the person, but the actual word. At the time the word God had not been etymologized. That is tracing back the origin. The relevance of this will also be mentioned later in the book.

Remember the section of the Old Testament about the prophets? Well yes, as discussed they prophesized about the continuous judgement of the Israelites. They prophesized about the cause of this continuous judgment on them. Their selfishness, self-righteousness and their unkind spirits. They also prophesized that because the Israelites and all of mankind just didn't get it and would never get it, God had to give everyone that last glimmer of hope. Jesus. But wait, not all Jewish persons do not believe in Jesus. Remember the books of Judges. The prophets told all that God could not just keep assigning judges to watch over the Israelites but he would send the final judge. Here are a few scriptures to support this statement.

"Behold, the days come, saith the LORD, that I will make a new covenant with the house of Israel, and with the house of Judah." Jeremiah 31:31(NIV)

"Therefore the Lord himself will give you sign: The virgin will conceive and give birth to a son: and will call him Immanuel" Isaiah 7:14 (NIV)

Why is this important? God will let things go on, without interference or judgement. He has decided to let man's free will, heart and love guide him or her their actions. And if man choses not to live a life or humanity or in service of others, they will be judged accordingly. And there will be one about to come who will judge our hearts.

Christ is prophesied in more than 200 prophecies in the Old Testament relating to his birth, life, death and resurrection. Too many times for me to have previously mentioned, But others, unbelievers or critical scholars, maintain that those prophecies have been written after Jesus death or adopted by Christian theology retroactively. Many of Jesus teachings were based on the times and the tradition of the Pharisees and traditional Jewish teachings. Jesus molded His teaching into a doctrine of love and non-retribution. It is important to remember that the Old Testament was focused on the "Law". God anointed individuals and nations of people to live according to these Laws. He also tried to let His children know they can make it easy just give Him his respect. Unfortunately God realized that "free will" made this almost impossible. So if He wanted His creation of man to continue HE would have to send someone to fulfill the Laws. Here comes the New Testament. The Testament that should define and separate Christians from other religions. Before we explore the New Testament please understand that after all the teaching of the Old Testament there still needed to be a Savoir. Why? Because no one got it. God still needed to have someone (HIS Son) consistently remind people who His Father was and is, and why everyone is getting it wrong.

We will now focus on the New Testament. The Testament of things to come. The Testament of Jesus Himself. I will review His life according to the Gospels, His miracles and parables. I will explain His purpose in the rest of the Testament.

Chapter Two

New Testament

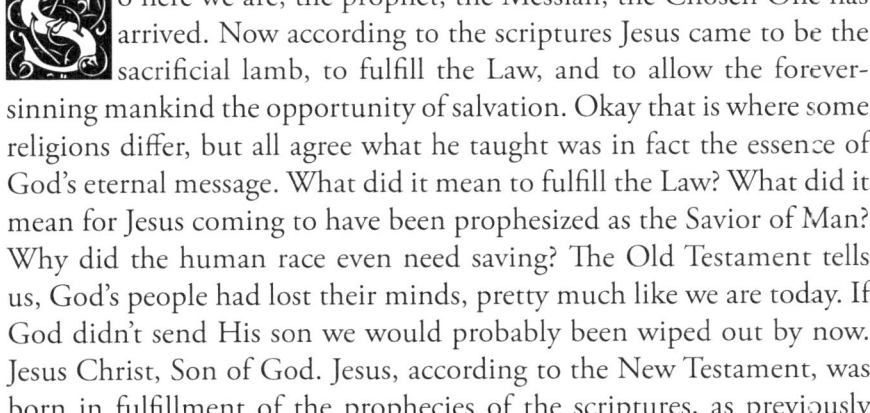

o here we are, the prophet, the Messiah, the Chosen One has arrived. Now according to the scriptures Jesus came to be the sacrificial lamb, to fulfill the Law, and to allow the forever-sinning mankind the opportunity of salvation. Okay that is where some religions differ, but all agree what he taught was in fact the essence of God's eternal message. What did it mean to fulfill the Law? What did it mean for Jesus coming to have been prophesized as the Savior of Man? Why did the human race even need saving? The Old Testament tells us, God's people had lost their minds, pretty much like we are today. If God didn't send His son we would probably been wiped out by now. Jesus Christ, Son of God. Jesus, according to the New Testament, was born in fulfillment of the prophecies of the scriptures, as previously discussed

The New Testament is a compilation of writings, which are divided into 27 twenty-seven separate works or books. Those 27 books are further divided into four sections. The Gospels, Acts, the Letters, and Revelations. Some say the New Testament is divided into five sections. The Gospels, Acts, Paul's Epistles and Hebrews, General Epistles and Revelations. I am going to use the former division.

The Gospels consist of the four narratives written by Matthew, Mark, Luke and John, of Jesus Christ's ministry and an actual account of Jesus life. Each gives their recount, their point of view of their time with Jesus. Matthew who was Jewish, tells the story aimed at a Jewish audience trying to convince them that Jesus was the prophesize Messiah. Mark's Gospel is an appeal to the average Greeks in a sermon sort of tone. He basically gives facts and puts the ball in the readers court to make the right choices and do the right thing. It serves as a motivational call to action and conversion that appeals to common Greeks. Luke's Gospel was written to more privileged and educated Greeks. Also Luke's audience were those next generations whom had only heard so-called fairy tales, but never had anything concrete to lean on and draw independent conclusions. Finally, the Gospel of John was written to already devoted, committed Christians in the Church that John founded and led whom struggled to understand the challenges set before them.

The Book of Acts or Acts of the Apostles recounts the early history of Christianity when the Apostles began to preach the Gospel. Some similarity but more focus on what happened after Jesus crucifixion.

Next are the Letters or Epistles. They were scripted mainly by Paul, who never knew or even met Jesus. They were written to specific churches in individual cities or addressed to individual persons. They letters or epistles contributed to Paul consist of the following books. Romans; I and II Corinthians; Galatians; Ephesians; Philippians; Colossians; I and II Thessalonians; I and II Timothy; Titus; and Philemon. Hebrews is arguably also one of the Epistles.

The next seven Books are the General Epistles. Unlike the Epistles written by Paul, they were not intended for specific churches, and generally accepted that they were named for the authors. They consist of James, 1 Peter, 2 Peter, 1 John, 2 John, 3 John and Jude.

The last book of the New Testament, Revelation, is an Apocalyptic prophecy, or an end of the world prophecy to make it simple. It is also technically the twenty-second epistle compilation of prophetic writings.

We are going to start with the Gospels. Because each was written through the eyes of the four disciples, the gospel all contains similarities. The Gospels tell of Jesus birth, parables, healing, preaching, miracles and of course crucifixion and resurrection. For simplicity I will briefly mention these physical miracles of Jesus and try to emphasis what Jesus said, whom He said it to and why. Oh, I will do the same for the disciples and Jesus followers when relative. But before we get into specific teachings, we will have a quick historical narrative, as written in the Gospels. I will try to keep this short so we may get to the teachings and ultimately the point of this book.

The Gospels of the New Testament begins with an account of the life of Jesus. As in all the Gospels Jesus goes from Capernaum to Galilee. A genealogy of Jesus is given, tracing His earthly father Joseph's lineage to Abraham. If you remember, the Bible is the genealogical story of one main family. It is the genealogy of Joseph, not Mary, that traced back to Abraham. After the genealogy there are various accounts of what Jesus did, and what Jesus said. This depends on the view point of either Matthew, Mark, Luke or John. The last chapters in three of the Gospels tell the story of the death and resurrection of Jesus. The Luke and Matthew accounts of the birth of Jesus have a number of points in common; both have Jesus being born in Bethlehem, in Judea, to a virgin mother. Luke's account details Joseph and Mary travel from their home in Nazareth for the census to Bethlehem, where Jesus is born and laid in a manger. The story we all know.

Jesus was born circa 6 B.C. in Bethlehem. His mother, Mary, was a virgin who was betrothed to Joseph, a carpenter. Christians believe Jesus was born through Immaculate Conception. His lineage can be traced back to the house of David. According to the Gospel of Matthew, Jesus was born during the reign of Herod the Great, who upon hearing of his birth felt threatened and tried to kill Jesus by ordering all of Bethlehem's male children under age two to be killed. But Joseph was warned by an angel and took Mary and the child to Egypt until Herod's death, where upon he brought the family back and settled in the town of Nazareth, in Galilee.

It is believed that he began his ministry at age thirty when he was baptized by John the Baptist, who upon seeing Jesus, declared him the Son of God. After baptism, Jesus went into the Judean desert to fast and meditate for 40 days and nights. During this time, Satan came to Jesus and tried to tempt him. But Jesus refused all of Satan's attempts. The Temptation of Christ is chronicled in the Gospels of Matthew, Mark and Luke. After winning or defeating Satan's temptations Jesus returned to Galilee and begin his ministry. Jesus wisely chooses His disciples, which will be discuss in more detail later. Jesus ministers. Judas then betrays him and Peter denies that he knows him. Pilate orders the death of Jesus. Jesus is mocked, beaten and crucified, between two thieves. He dies and is buried in the tomb of Joseph of Arimathaea. Christ is resurrected and appears to Mary Magdalene, then to others. Then Jesus chooses the seventy disciples whom he sends to preach. The Seventy Disciples or Seventy-two were early followers of Jesus mentioned in the Gospel of Luke. According to Luke, the only gospel in which they appear, Jesus appointed them and sent them out in pairs on a specific mission which is detailed in the text. Jesus or The Holy Spirit enabled them to speak in all tongues as they need to communicate with foreigners. You can surmise what you wish about this interpretation of "speaking in tongues". He ascends into heaven.

Well, that's the short historical overview. Let me quickly introduce Jesus disciples before we dive into what Jesus, preached, taught and how He lived. In the Books Matthew, Mark and Luke Jesus began searching for His disciples. The first two were brothers Simon called Peter and Andrew. The next two disciples were also two brothers, James and John. With those four Jesus began to perform miracles. Later Jesus kind of recruited eight more. They were Philip, Bartholomew, Thomas, Matthew, James, Thaddeus, Simon and Judas. I could tell your stories about each, but it would not really add to my point. Other than it is important for everyone to know why Jesus chose each one. The gathering and mentoring of the disciples are throughout the Gospels. They are known in some scripture as The Twelve. Many people believe the Apostle Paul was a disciple. But he was not. He was in fact, considered one of the most influential of the group besides Peter. Something important to know is that they were each unique. In fact, a few of them were unbelievers who turned their lives around and committed to and followed Jesus. With all His disciples. Jesus began to performed certain miracles. Crowds began to follow Him and thus He began to prepare His disciples and teach them what it is they needed to know. What they needed to know is what we should know. Why? Because being a Christian is about being a disciple. I feel this is one of the most important attributes of Christianity, that millions do not see understand or even attempt.

The Gospels also tell of Jesus healings, miracles and parables. The miracles of Jesus are the unexplainable, non-human sort of supernatural deeds done by Jesus. Just a quick note, these deeds are in both Christian and Islamic texts. We do however lean toward Judaism as a "brother" religion. The majority of these miracles are faith healings, exorcisms, resurrection and control over nature. The first of the signs or miracles was Jesus changing water into wine at Cana. This appears in the Book of John. There were also many cases of healing. I will just list a few.

The earliest is a story of the healing of a blind man in Bethsaida in the Gospel of Mark. The Gospel of John describes an episode in which Jesus heals a man blind from birth. Mark's Gospel has an account of the healing of a man named Bartimaeus. The Gospel of Luke tells the same story of Jesus healing an unnamed blind man, done as Jesus is leaving Jericho. A story in which Jesus cures a leper appears in Matthew, Mark and Luke. Also in these three

Books Jesus heals a cripple (sorry, a disabled gentleman). The man was brought to Jesus on a mat and Jesus told him to get up and walk. Jesus then told the man that his sins were forgiven. There were of course many more. Throughout the Gospels Jesus healed many men and women. Sinful, pious, demon filled and even Herod. You should all know who Herod was. Then we have numerous other healings, raising of the dead and the exorcism of many supposedly demon possessed individuals. I will leave it up to you to read more detail about whom Jesus healed and why. I will point out that you should pay very, very close attention to whom He healed.

There was also many other acts of miracles performed by Jesus. These were of the miraculous worldly nature. Here are a few. All of them well known.

Throughout the Gospels Jesus feeds the multitudes. There are either different accounts or similar miracles, just recounted differently. There is the "Feeding of the 5,000", is reported by all four gospels, Matthew; Mark Luke and John. This is also known as the "miracle of the five loaves and two fishes. Just for knowledge sake, there a two different accounts of Jesus feeding a multitude. Another well known miracle is when Jesus stilled or calmed the storm. You know the story. Jesus wan on a small boat with His crew when a tremendous storm came which broke their boat. While the disciples were panicking, Jesus was completely chill and even sleeping. The disciples woke him and said to him, "Teacher, don't you care if we drown?" Jesus looked at them rolled His eyes. Now that is just my dramatization. Jesus demanded the storm to be still. And it was. The disciples looked at Jesus and asked was He afraid. Jesus laughed at them, called them little children and questioned their faith. And we all know the story of Jesus walking on water in John. Again, faith is the main lesson or point.

Why are the miracles performed by Jesus important? Many think they add to the mystery or supernatural powers of Christ. Many view the miracles of Jesus as acts of power and omnipotence, but I do not believe Jesus did anything to prove a point. I am of the belief Jesus performed blessings to others as a show of love and mercy, to show compassion for sinful and suffering humanity. We must take not and remember all Jesus healing and miracles were for people less fortunate, in need or occasionally just to show mercy.

The Gospels also show how the priests opposed Jesus. One of the most pertinent parts of and the progression of the Gospels is when Jesus reproves the Pharisees for their false traditions and ceremonies. Jesus consulted for all to beware of the Pharisees. It is something that must be read and even more importantly be comprehended. Jesus also ate with publicans and sinners. Publicans were similar to today's city workers. They collected taxes and managed municipal projects. This is important and reoccurring. One more time, who Jesus chose to associate with should be noticed. All of these points and teachings will be revisited throughout the book, because they all are important to the founding, development and current state of America.

Jesus speaks of blasphemy against the Holy Ghost, and identifies those who believe, as his family. Would mocking the Holy Spirit be a form a blasphemy. Would faking speaking in the Holy Spirit be mocking or blasphemy? Would convincing people they are speaking in tongues for a greater offering be blasphemy? Jesus sends out the Twelve. His twelve multi- lingual disciples. To do what? Become rich through tithes? No, to teach His words and introduce people to salvation.

Jesus preaches the condemnation of those who offend his little ones. What? Those who offend his little ones? One more, what!!! Where has this surfaced in today's news? He invites little children to come unto him and teaches them how to gain eternal life. Jesus love, respect and admiration for children should be noted. Quite frankly, it should make pedophile loving Christians really, really scared of their ending to come. The protection and stewardship of children is also a repeated theme in the bible as well as a very important one.

Next, let us briefly discuss parables. Jesus travels teaching and ministering many times using parables. I will quickly sum up a few parables Jesus gives the parable of the wicked husbandmen. Jesus gives the parables of the lost sheep, of the piece of silver, and of the prodigal son. Jesus teaches, "Repent or perish". He gives the parable of the barren fig tree likens the kingdom of God to a mustard seed. He discusses whether few or many are saved, and laments over Jerusalem. He teaches humility, and gives the parable of the great supper. Jesus gives a few more parables. There are actually about thirty or more. A few to mention were the parables of the unjust judge, of the Pharisee and publican, and the parable of the wicked husbandmen Jesus gives the parable of the unjust steward and the parable of the rich man and Lazarus. Jesus also speaks of offenses, forgiveness, and faith and as a reoccurring message, He says there shall be false Christs and false prophets. The mentioning of false prophets is mentioned several times in the New Testament and by the end of this chapter you should have an idea where I am going.

One more thing I will point out consistent with the Gospels.

We can now begin with the individual Books of the New Testament. I will try to focus on the substantive the coloring book stories. As previously stated the first Book of the New Testament is Matthew. It is in this Book we read about the first teachings of Jesus. Here are the first teachings or sermon of Jesus to His disciples and a multitude. Matthew 5:3-10 (NIV)

"Blessed are the poor in spirit, for theirs is the kingdom of heaven"

"Blessed are the those who mourn, for the will be comforted"

"Blessed are the meek, for they will inherit the earth"

"Blessed are those who hunger and thirst for righteousness, for they will be filled"

"Blessed are the merciful, for they will be shown mercy"

"Blessed are the pure in heart, for they shall see God"

"Blessed are the peacemakers, for they will be called sons of God"

"Blessed are those who are persecuted because of righteousness, for theirs is the kingdom of heaven"

Now Jesus did not say you would not see the kingdom of heaven if you did not have any of the qualifying beatitudes. But let me ask you, are the rich, selfish, unrighteous, unmerciful and inhumane, more likely to see the kingdom of heaven. Just asking. Jesus said Blessed are those... Blessed. One more time.. Blessed. Is being blessed about riches?. If you think so, well, do not. Please understand, according to the scripture in the New Testament you can be poor and extremely blessed. Would you say America represents those poor in spirit? What about those in mourning, peacemakers, meek, or pure in heart? What about righteous? Are Christians in America persecuted because of their stand for God? We have had many persecuted for telling the truth and standing up for justice. Why are peaceful protesters for humanity "destroyed" while hate groups are praised? Jesus clearly says how one should live in order to be blessed. Did the Beatitudes correspond to the Old Testament scripture of being humble, caring for the poor, and being delivered from suffering? Rhetorical.

Jesus talks about not swearing. Many Christians profess, "I do not swear". But they forget the reason Jesus said this. Read Matt 5:37. Any version of the Bile will do. Jesus goes on to qualify His statement. "Simply let your "yes" be "yes" and your "no" be "no". Let your word stand on its own. Do not lie. The essence of swearing is not cursing or intended to be generically using God's name, but using the name of a divine entity to validate the truthfulness of ones' statement or comment. An example is swearing on the Bible, so help you God. I will add my personal take on lying. A lie is basically intentionally making someone think something that is not true. That can occur many different ways and at least fifty ways it can refer to one's body language, falsely using sex to convey feelings, saying to someone "OK, go with that" or "What do you believe? All to convey or sway someone into believing a falsehood. Get my point? The lie is you intentionally having a person walk away believing in something that is not true. That is a lie. When your lie lead to any kind of harm, physically, emotionally or spiritually there will be a price to pay. I will drive this point into the ground later, so be ready. Okay apologies, let us move on.

Another principle in Matthew is "Love for your enemies". Do not just love those who love you. Greet those other than you as a brother. Anyone, not just those who loves you. Bullies as well as a certain past President love those who love them. And, to keep everything one hundred, I fail at this. I try but sometimes I just cannot take it and respond to evil. I feel an important precursor to this is understanding you shouldn't have enemies. If you do, you should try to make amends or correct, before you choose hate. Also we as humans seem to hate either what we do not understand or hate those who are different. So I guess my point is stop hating!

The next principle is "Giving to the needy". Jesus taught that all we are given in life is a gift, and we should share with others less fortunate. For all those who think they earned every dime by hard work and do not think they should help others, well you're a waste of life. Jesus didn't say brag about it or tell everyone how you gave a donation. . But He did add, "but do so with your heart". Do not brag about it, do not boast about it, do not tell everyone on a televised show how much you gave to the poor. Jesus also counsels the rich young man. "If you want to be truly saved, go, sell your possessions and give to the poor, and you will have treasure in heaven. Then come, follow me". Why is this important? Another principle is, "Do not get caught up in wealth and worldly treasures". What!? Isn't that the whole point to Capitalism?

Looking at the Book of Mark there was something I purposefully left out or did not mention when giving an overview of the Gospels. Do you know what led to Jesus arrest and subsequent crucifixion?

One day while Jesus is in Jerusalem, in the market place of the temple. He sees them selling books, CD's, planes and yachts. No actually idols, doves and other items.

Mark reads… "On reaching Jerusalem, Jesus entered the temple courts and began driving out those who were buying and selling there. He overturned the tables of the money changers and the benches of those selling doves, and would not allow anyone to carry merchandise through the temple courts. And as He taught them, and as He said in Mark 11:17 (NIV), "Is it not written: 'My house will be called a house of prayer for all nations'? But you have made it 'a den of robbers.' "The chief priests and the teachers of the law heard this and began looking for a way to kill him, for they feared him, because the whole crowd was amazed at his teaching" I cannot express the importance of this enough. The selling of merchandise is what caused Jesus to have His ultimate fit. Do I really need to explain or give today's examples?

The Gospels tend to emphasize the intensity of Jesus teachings. Further scripture emphasizes the need for the truth as well as love, because they are one in the same. Does anyone disagree? Christian or not? Does anyone not believe this is what Jesus taught? Religious left or right. Evangelical or sensible. Can anyone dispute this? As a reoccurring message, He says there shall be false Christs and false prophets. The mentioning of false prophets is mentioned several times in the New Testament and by the end of this chapter you should have an idea where I am going.

As we continue to search the Gospels we see that in the book of Luke, Jesus teaches his disciples that the need for Christian love is great. Jesus stresses to his followers that they must love the unlovely as well as those that appeal to them. Jesus was saying that the love which discipleship demands, like the love of God, extends to those who do not deserve it.

This love principle should extend to your enemies, to those who hate you, to those who curse you, and to those who abuse you. Jesus introduces the Lord's Prayer as He continues casting out of devils.

This book also emphasizes baptisms. We are introduced to John the Baptist who both preached and baptizes Jesus. And upon His baptism God declared Jesus was His Son. Not equal, but Son. The book also traces genealogy back to Adam. A point emphasized in the previous chapter,

After verses about Jesus fasts, being tempted by the devil, but instead of the story where God made a bet with the devil sitting chilling, Jesus cast out devils. One disciple named Peter called the fisherman, and soon to be major religious figure was called to be a catcher of men. Save men if you do not follow. He pronounces that those whom are obedient will be blesses and there will be woes upon the wicked, the wicked will eventually lead to cautions of false prophets.

He reprehends the Pharisees and says the blood of the righteous shall be required of that evil generation. Jesus teaches main points. We should beware of hypocrisy, layup treasures in heaven, rather than on earth, prepare for the coming of the Lord, where much is given, much is required and I must highlight, preaching the gospel causes division.

Jesus foretells the destruction of the temple and of Jerusalem. Again if you remember this is crucial as it was a major reoccurring issue in the Old Testament. He tells of the signs to precede his Second Coming, and once again gives the parable of the fig tree.

Christ institutes the sacrament. What is a sacrament and why was it important? A sacrament is something done to solidify one's devotion or commitment to an ideology. In this case, a religious ideology. Like a baptism, taking communion or later in history reciting the Nicene Creed. You should all know what those "emblem" things are. Beware of partaking unworthily.

Jesus then suffers in Gethsemane and is betrayed and arrested. Peter denies knowing him and Christ is smitten and mocked. Just more repetition.

Luke strongly ties the right use of riches to discipleship; and securing heavenly treasure is linked with caring for the poor, the naked and the hungry, for God is supposed to have a special interest in the poor. This theme is consistent with God's protection and care of the poor in the Old Testament.

As we move on let us look at the Book of John.

"In the beginning there was the word..." I emphasize this because many Christians use this to justify their false teaching that Jesus is God. Does God have a beginning? No, he does not. Christ is the Word of God. Purposed to fulfill God's Word at the beginning. He created all things and was made flesh. Why? So we could all hear and see the Word. Not that relevant to purpose of book or end game, but thought I would say. Something very close to my understanding of who Jesus was and I found or find amazing was Jesus washed the feet of the Twelve. I have only heard of this being done once by someone in my lifetime. Stay tuned. You may be shocked. Jesus identifies Judas as his betrayer and He commands the disciples to love one another. And of course Jesus is betrayed, arrested crucified, and buried in the tomb of Joseph of Arimathaea.

The Book of Acts is important because it forms a bridge connecting what Jesus and what the apostles' taught. It also give us a glance of the establishment of the church. The Book of Acts enables the reader to understand the growth of the church in its beginning with each succeeding age. This also allows the reader to gain an understanding of the principles that ought to govern all church to come. Acts shows us how the work of Jesus teachings, the Holy Spirit and the apostles help the beginning and spread of the church. In its infancy things looked promising.

As previously mentioned the next group of Books are the Epistles or Letters. Paul mainly wrote them. A quick note about Paul. Paul was not a disciple nor did he ever meet Jesus. Actually his name was originally Saul and feared for his persecution of disciples and Christians. I am sure everyone knew that already. Like most New Testament letters, this letter is known by the name of the recipients, the church of Roman. Romans teaches the gospel is the power of God unto salvation through Jesus Christ. Paul wrote this letter to express his enthusiasm for their success and his desire to visit them personally. The bulk of the letter, however, is a deep and poignant study on the basic doctrines of the Christian faith. Paul emphasized that God shall render to every man according to his deeds. According to his deeds. It is insane that some falsely teach that your actions do not matter. What deeds would you say the United States has done? Good or bad? Good or bad according to who? God? Jesus? Our fore fathers? Our former president?

Roman teaches that both Jews and Gentiles were judged by gospel laws. But Jesus teaches that man is not justified by the law of Moses. I repeat, both Jew and Gentile. We cannot buy God's favor by tithing or back then sacrifices. He teaches that man is justified by faith, which should manifest itself through righteous works. Man will basically be judged according to one's faith or actions and belief in Christ. A known verse is "the wages of sin is death"

Paul attempts to get his readers to understand Jesus came to fulfill the Law. We should understand that, embrace it and live up to it, by our actions and way of life. Understanding this makes us sort of adopted sons of God. God's elect. Who are God's elect? All through the Bible we read who God and Jesus favored. Christ makes intercession for man. Jesus took the beating and Jesus did the dying. But, when it is all said and done we better live up to it. Those who believe God's word should avoid strife and unrighteous judgment of each other.

During the Bible we have noticed that the Israelites where crowned as the chosen people. But they continually hardened their hearts against it. Romans gives attention to the Gentiles. Or us. But whether we live in the world of Jews or Gentiles we all lost our minds!

One last thing, Paul salutes divers saints. It is not my main point but it is very important. The divers saints are the many gifts of the spirit. They all come from the Holy Spirit. They are all equally special and important. There is one gift that is exploited.

'Speaking in tongues can be easily exploited, I asked for the spirit of discernment. That is a separate manuscript.

Paul counsels the saints who cause divisions and tells saints to avoid those who cause divisions. Things like denominations and strife about who is right and who is wrong.

In First and Second Corinthians Paul took a great interest in the churches spread throughout the region of Corinth. Because the city of Corinth was corrupt with all kinds of immorality, so Paul instructed to this church to refrain from sinful practices and remain united as Christians in thought. As throughout the New Testament Paul urges the saints to be united in the same mind and in the same judgment. Basically there should not be hundreds of divisions. With wisdom Paul tells that both a saint and a weak simpleton preach the gospel but only the saint will save souls. How do you know a soul has been saved? That could probably be another manuscript. Brothers should not argue scripture with each other. The gospel is preached by the power of the Spirit and should not be equated with the Second Amendment. The Spirit reveals all things to the saints. This will be mentioned again. Many so-called saints and preachers lived and taught the masses by reciting words and just plain yapping, Paul teaches the Kingdom of God is not about vane yapping but in power. Power to live as an example to others. And most of the time this means not living like others.

Paul praised acts of self-discipline as he also rejoiced in his Christian liberty. Like Jesus he freely preached the Gospel to all free of charge. But that was back then. Paul provided contrasts between true and false sacraments. Just like he and many others provided reveals of false and true prophets. Paul also praised the high status of charity. He taught that charity was born of the heart and an act of pure love. Paul also said that charity excels and exceeds almost all else. For our inner spiritual growth and witnessing, Paul touched on something else. The desire to have spiritual gifts. I briefly mentioned this. Where most Christians claim to have the gift of speaking in tongues. Paul told everyone that the gift of prophecy is the greater gift. This is what I mentioned and is spelled out. Paul continued his counseling, to stand fast in the faith and let all things be done with charity.

In short, there are two main topics of instruction. The Saints and the Holy Spirit. The Saints are expected to be whom God intended then to be, truthful and take guidance from the Holy Spirit. Satan sends forth false apostles, the Saints cannot be false, Do we have Saints today?

Galatians. Paul founded, the church of Galatian and after a few years continued his missionary journeys. During his absence a groups of false teachers corrupted the Galatians by claiming that Christians must continue to observe the different laws from the Old Testament. When Paul returned he appealed for them to return to the doctrine of Jesus Christ and to avoid the practices of false teachers. There were Saints and there were preachers. Paul warned of those preaching false gospels. He added we should bear one's burden. We reap what we sow be not weary in doing well or good. To explain the "be not weary", basically don't give up as you wait for good things to happen. God gave the gospel to Abraham passed it through Israel on to Christ.

Paul calls the Galatians back to Christ and compares the two covenants. Last but not least, one of the most important things is it is in this book where the "Fruits of the Spirit" are introduced. Not to be confused with the "Gifts of the Holy Spirit" Paul's letter to the Ephesians as with Galatians emphasizes God's grace and the fact that human beings cannot attain salvation through works or legalism. He is not talking about faith with works or being faithful by deeds. Paul is saying that man cannot invent ways or do acts of good deeds, to erase inhumanity, instead of consciously doing the right things or being righteous. We are supposed to have faith when the Saints tell us we were saved by grace. Not by acting like fanatically and preaching that our grace can be bought, recited or demanded. Paul reemphasizes Christ saves Jew and Gentile alike. Gentiles are fellow heirs with Israel. The fact that all humanity are God's heirs or children is repeated throughout and very important as we as a nation fail to remember this. The Book tell us that servants and masters are judged by the same law. No need to further explain.

Philippians. While the major theme of Ephesians is grace, the major theme of the letter to the Philippians is joy. Paul encouraged the Philippian Christians to relish the joy of living as servants of God. One tie to explaining to masters, all are servants. He also said that we should all be disciples of Jesus Christ. Paul, was confined in Roman prison cell while writing it.

Paul faced martyrdom and stayed true to living like a Saint. Paul sacrifices all things for Christ to set examples of righteousness.

Colossians is another letter Paul wrote as a prisoner in Rome and another in which Paul sought to correct numerous false teachings that had infiltrated the church. This time the Church was preaching that Jesus Christ was not fully God and began worshiping angels and other beings. Throughout Colossians, Paul speaks of Jesus divinity, and His rightful place as Head of the church and Firstborn of the Father. The practice of worshiping or exalting angels and other so-called saints would still become a problem later is the Christian history.

In First and Second Thessalonians Paul visited the Greek city of Thessalonica during his second missionary journey, he received a report from Timothy and was concerned about the health of the congregation. Since Paul was about to be persecuted he sent the letter to clarify some points on which the church members were confused. In the letter we know as 2 Thessalonians, Paul reminded the people of the need to continue living and working as followers of God until Christ returned. Thessalonian's teach that the gospel comes both in word and in power. Jesus taught this by examining the "Saints". Or those who profess to be Saints. What do I mean by examined? True ministers preach in a godly manner. They develop disciples and converts become joyful missionaries. They are sheep who go out and become herders. They must go out and teach the truth as Jesus taught. They are not supposed to sit under the minister or pastors forever for churches' financial stability. True Saints recognize their short comings, their demons and strive to overcome them. They strive to be good examples and do not take advantage of their flock. They never and I mean never display feeling of superiority or condemnation.

Paul tells the Thessalonian's that the Lord Jesus will take vengeance upon the ungodly. A reoccurring message. Hopefully we know by now who Jesus labeled as ungodly.

The books we know as 1 and 2 Timothy were the first epistles written to individuals, rather than regional congregations. Timothy had been taught by his mentor Paul for years and sent him to lead the growing church in Ephesus. For that reason, Paul's epistles to Timothy contain practical advice for pastoral ministry. His teachings included instruction on proper doctrine, how to avoid unnecessary debates, the order of worship during gatherings, qualifications for church leaders, amongst other things. The letter we know as 2 Timothy is quite personal and offers encouragement regarding Timothy's faith and ministry as a servant of God.

Paul discusses how Christ sees everything and is our mediator to God. He also discusses how woman should carry themselves, to continue in faith, charity, holiness. But as previously mentioned Paul wrote mainly to Timothy, setting forth qualifications for bishops and deacons. He emphasized that Saints were to care for their poor and for the elderly. A specific call and a specific duty. Paul continued to teach of the reality of things once were and things to come. He spoke that the love of money is the root of all evil. Everyone should fight the good fight of faith and most of all not trust in worldly riches. Everyone should shun contention and seek godliness.

A very important and prophetic scripture in 2nd Timothy 3:2-4. Taken from the NIV Bible.

People will be lovers of themselves, lovers of money, boastful, proud, abusive, disobedient to their parents, ungrateful, unholy, without love, unforgiving, slanderous, without self-control, brutal, not lovers of the good, treacherous, rash, conceited, lovers of pleasure rather than lovers of God"

Titus was also a protégé of Paul's who had been sent to lead a church located on the island of Crete. Once again, this letter contains a mix of leadership advice and personal encouragement. The churches on Crete were just as susceptible to false teachers as any other church, so Paul directed Titus to establish a group of faithful elders to oversee the doctrinal purity and good conduct of the believers on Crete.

Paul gave instructions to Titus about the roles of specific groups of people, older men, older women, young women, young men, and slaves, as well as general instructions to all believers about their conduct. We must remember slavery was not condoned but a part of the times then and to come. Paul taught everyone should do what is right according to their own demographic or station.

This book is Epistle of Paul to Philemon and one of the shortest in the Bible. It was written by Paul, while imprisoned. Paul wrote this letter to Philemon, a wealthy Christian. It is basically a plea for a runaway slave It was written on behalf of Onesimus, a runaway slave who had wronged his owner Philemon. It is assumed that Onesimus stole money. At some point Onesimus came into contact with Paul. It is not clear if he was arrested and imprisoned alongside Paul or heard of Paul and searched for him. That said, Onesimus became a Christian believer. Even though they got closer Paul considered it better to send him back to Philemon with an accompanying letter. which suggested they bond and reconcile as Christian brothers. The gospel is remembered as one that changes a servant into a brother.

Now please do not think this is one of the many books of the Bible condoning slavery. Paul wrote the letter to request or recommend that Onesimus was treated like a brother. With respect and justly. Being consistent he said the slave should honor his current obligation that fell upon him. It is like Jesus commanding that citizens pay taxes or give to Caesar as you should.

Jesus was not saying slavery or taxes were just. He was saying have faith, honor our obligation and be the best person you can honoring God. Don't sweat and make promises you don't intend to keep.

The book of Hebrews compares and contrasts Jesus to key historical people and events from the Old Testament. Through these comparisons, we see His superiority. He is greater than angels, the Torah, Moses, the Promised Land, priests, Melchizedek, sacrifices, and the covenant. He is God's Word, the hope for a new creation, our eternal priest, and the perfect sacrifice.

The Book of Hebrews addresses the believers in Christ, unbelievers whom accepted the facts of Christ, and unbelievers who were aware of Christ, but ultimately rejected Him. It is important to understand which group is being addressed in which passage. To fail to do so can cause us to draw conclusions inconsistent with the rest of Scripture.

Throughout the book, we are also reminded to remain faithful to Jesus and follow great models of faith from the Old Testament despite hardships and persecution. These challenges will make us uncomfortable but instead of fearing them embrace them for the strength they bring.

Remaining faithful to the Old Testament means be faithful to God, not act pious or holy.

Jesus is the ultimate revelation of God's love and mercy and is worthy of all our trust and devotion.

Hebrews remind readers about all the major Saints and prophets of the Old Testament.

Paul draws the conclusion that those in the Old Testament were bringing us to God. They were the authors of the book that was started. Jesus is the completion or finisher of that faith.

The Epistle of James was written by Albert. Just joking. Of course, it was written by James. The letter was supposedly written to "the twelve tribes scattered abroad". The twelve tribes probably refer to the entire Jewish nation. James's epistle is a practical guide to living the Christian life. One of the most important themes of this epistle is for Christians to reject hypocrisy and favoritism. The Book of James instructs us how to recognize pure religion, and if you if lack wisdom, ask of God. Many folks should be asking God and not relying on the TV dude. However, above all else resist temptation and be doers of the word.

It is once again told that God chose the poor of this world to be rich in faith. We are also reminded that "Faith without works is dead". Yapping about how much you love scripture, how much you give in tithes or photo-ops with a Bible, will not gain you favor with God.

James also gets a little more specific and tells us that only if we watch our tongue will we gain perfection. Heavenly wisdom is pure, peaceable, and full of mercy.

He also reminds us the world is in direct opposition to God and misery awaits the prideful rich.

First and Second Peter. Peter was also a primary leader in the early church, especially in Jerusalem. Like Paul, Peter wrote his epistles while under arrest as a prisoner in Rome. And his words teach about the reality of suffering and persecution for followers of Jesus. Peter's second epistle also contains strong warnings against different false teachers who were attempting to lead the church astray. A repeated and monumental lesson to be ignored, even today.

Peter reemphasizes that we are in subjection to the laws of man. Don't have to like them, we may not respect them, but we had better obey them. Obey them. Do not twist them. Do not abuse or use them to disenfranchise others.

Husbands and wives should honor each other. He mentions and reminds us that the righteous will be tried and tested, in all things. Did you ever wonder why good people go through so many trials and why the grimy idiot seems to skate through life? Be happy if you are tested. Peter revisits how men who are as identified as saints better live by God's standards being humble in all they do and achieve. He states false teachers among the saints are damned and lustful saints will perish in their own corruption. This applies to politicians as well.

Written around A.D. 90, the epistles First, Second and Third John are among the last books written in the New Testament. Because they were written after the fall of Jerusalem during the first waves of Roman persecution for Christians. These letters were intended as encouragement and guidance for Christians living in a hostile world. Though probably less hostile to some than others today. One of the major themes of John's writing is the reality of God's love and the truth that our experiences with God should push us to love one another. Saints gain fellowship with God by obedience. In order to get this point across John reminds us to stay truthful, respectful and live as Jesus wanted us to live. He makes a point of telling us the consequences of being a deceitful liar. A major reoccurring point is we must watch out for and ward off those who are liars and those who falsely teach hatred, bigotry and attach themselves to riches and division. John was adamant on making these points because he was telling of the end of days.

Now I will not dwell on that as not to lose any of my readers. But we must take heed to his warning of deceitful and lying people. As well as those who hurt, mislead and abuse the less fortunate and those seeking justice.

John tells us that if you are one of those so-called leaders you must confess your sins to gain forgiveness. And I am not talking about "hail Mary". I am talking the full confession, twelve step, teary eyed, begging for forgiveness and making true amends. Yes, this is mentioned or referenced throughout the New Testament.

Jude is a very short book. But one of my favorite. It was written by disciple or apostle Jude who according to scholars as the brother of James. So what is the book of Jude about? Well Jude focuses on two main points. One, a very common theme was false prophets, teachers and preachers whom claimed to be men of God. The second point was encouraging Christians to stand firm in Jesus words, not man's and fight for the truth.

The Book of Revelation is a hard Book to summarize. It is the last Book of the New Testament as well as the last book in the Bible. And I guess, it should be! I will assume Christian or not we have all heard of Revelations, of the Apocalypse. The book of Revelation is an apocalyptic or doomsday letter, which was written to seven churches as both encouragement and a warning. John supposedly wrote this Book. It tells of his visions or his dreams. I believe there is a difference. John's visions reveal that Jesus will one day have a dramatic return the end of the world is coming because no one took heed to the words of the Bible. No one took heed to all the preaching, the scriptures and the teachings. Revelation will come to pass as the final strike for our inhumanity. Now you may say that you personally are not inhumane. But unfortunately if the masses are or the government is or those making the decision that ruin the earth then it is a third strike.

I will try to sum this final Book up as well as I can, without being to wordy.

It begins with John, addressing the "Seven Churches of Asia". Through a series of letters John reveals his visions, including of figures such as the Seven-Headed Dragon, the Serpent, and the Beast, which culminate in the Second Coming of Jesus. Not much and then too much to talk about. First God tried destroying the wicked and their land by really harsh means, as well as the wicked person's children's children. Then He tried to have Jesus get His point across. And then He decided, "what the heck". They do not get it. The Apocalypse, Armageddon, Revelation. I guess God is just going to let us duke it out. And I ain't mad at Him! Nowhere does God or Jesus mention other religions, just bad people. I am quite sure Jesus has a heavy heart. Let the apocalypse come. I will try to continue so we can read about the governments and religions whom will assure this prophecy.

The Bible is comprised of sixty-six Books. Thirty - nine Books in the Old Testament and Twenty seven Books in the New Testament. Keep in mind this is the Protestant Bible for the Catholic and Orthodox each have more Old Testament Books. But for our discussion we focused on the Protestant version, which breaks down into about eleven thousand one hundred and ninety chapters and over thirty one hundred verses. I make this point to acknowledge the fact that I omitted hundreds of historical references and thousands of verses. My goal to point out the underlining purpose of the things taught. In short, the New Testament though filled with what many called stories, fables and tales, it does have a common theme. Jesus came so God would basically give us a second chance. That second chance was not as much to live a sacred, perfect holy life, but to live a life of service, decency filled with love, respect and humanity. Remember Christians believe Jesus life was prophesized, and if they believe wholly in their divine book should also believe He came to accomplish those things, which He said He would..

There are a few main principles which Jesus drove home, throughout His ministry. One, he taught that His followers orthodox Jews, the Pharisees, Saducces and all should live good lives showing devotion to the scriptures, and all humanity. The Pharisees were similar in actions to many "far-right Christians. They talked the talk, while ignoring the humanity, democracy and freedom of all men. They believed in wearing fancy clothes and Jesus warned that those professing to be anointed by God should not to be false prophets and lead people astray. Another thing Jesus taught was the foolish aspirations for wealth, without the willingness to give it all away for the sake of your fellow man is an express ticket to HELL. Three, all fancy "garb", wealth, high falutin positions, fancy names, and all the rituals mean nothing in God's eyes. Four, the most important of all, Jesus said the Christian was to love and do good unto all men. It is evident in the Testaments that all men, Jew, Gentile, slave, prostitute and fisherman had a place in Jesus heart. Jesus taught that a Christian should never refrain from giving, to meet a need, out of a love for his possessions. He also taught that a believer is to live in readiness to give or lend without the thought of repayment or reward. This includes the reward of praise or acknowledgement. Nothing in this world is more valuable or precious than the soul of every man. Nothing is more important for man to be filled with love. For the person who does not love does not know God, for God is love. I am sure my readers know this. And there is no mistake about how love is defined. But will this message survive, will it blossom, will it even be considered?

The New Testament says that Jesus will be our final judge. That He will separate the sheep from the wolves. Many Christians preach that this separation is only based on one's profession of Christianity. That is hogwash! It is based on whether or not the person acts in a manner commensurate with the teaching of His father. Do you think He will do so with joy or sorrow in His heart? More on that later. After Jesus crucifixion the world would have to rely on those who tried to continue the message of Jesus, those who would twist that message and those who would out right ignore Jesus message. The message was not the laws of nations. The message was not to raise up self-proclaimed kings and rulers. The message was not to invade and conquer. The message was not to judge the validity of one's dominance, power or righteousness by the amount of gold and riches they have. Let me move on because we need to make the relationship between the change in Christianity and our ultimately the effect on our nation.

Chapter Three

After Crucifixion

esus has been crucified, risen and ascended into heaven. For most scholars and persons whom can read, this was the actual beginning of Christianity. For while Jesus was alive He insisted that people do not praise Him. After the resurrection of Jesus, the apostles or disciples spread the word of Jesus. What happens next? Do the words of Jesus spread? Does God's plan to redeem man-kind through His son's unselfish act of salvation blossom and fill the hearts of all men? Well, we know of the chaos that the world endured. And then again there is the Book of Revelation and the apocalypse waiting around the corner. Why should you believe all the chapters of the Bible or other religious text and not believe the very last chapter? If you believe in the last chapter then I guess my questions about the Jesus being pleased with His namesake is rhetorical. One quick note. The New Testament was actually written after Jesus crucifixion.

Let us very briefly discuss what happened to the twelve Apostles after the crucifixion of Jesus.

The apostles went far and wide to teach the message of the risen Christ. Certain teaching says they divided up the world to determine who would go where, so all could hear about Jesus. Speaking in the native tongues of the peoples, they ministered. They never wavered, never approved of the monarchies unjust rule and never approved of the false teachings of those proclaiming to be God's divine prophets and holy men. They suffered greatly for their faith and in most cases met violent deaths because of their witness and confessions. Many wonder how the 12 apostles died, but The New Testament tells of the fate of only two of the apostles: Judas, who betrayed Jesus went out and hanged himself, and James the son of Zebedee, was executed by Herod about 44 AD. This is in Acts.

PETER and PAUL were both martyred in Rome about 66 AD, during the persecution under Emperor Nero. Paul whom as stated was not one of the original disciples was beheaded. Peter was crucified, upside down at his request, since he did not feel he was worthy to die in the same manner as his Lord. But before they died the apostles tried to spread the words of their Christ. And their effort led them to be the two single greatest influences of religion today. The bible contains evidence that Peter was to be the Minister to the Jews and Paul the minister to the gentiles. This would indicate that they possessed equal positions within the early church. We will come back to the world wide affect the two had on modern day Christianity

ANDREW went to the "land of the man-eaters," in what is now the Soviet Union. Christians there claim him as the first to bring the gospel to their land. He also preached in Asia Minor, modern-day Turkey, and in Greece, where he is said to have been crucified.

THOMAS was probably most active in the area east of Syria. Let me mention something I forgot earlier. There are two facts about Thomas I wish to highlight. When Jesus decided to return to Judea, Thomas told the disciples they should all go and share the same fate. He was loyal. On the other hand, he actually helped coin the phrase "doubting Thomas". After Jesus crucifixion, Thomas doubted that Jesus had in fact, been resurrected. Tradition has Thomas preaching as far east as India, where the ancient Marthoma Christians revere him as their founder. They claim that he died there when pierced through with the spears of four soldiers.

PHILIP possibly had a powerful ministry in Carthage in North Africa and then in Asia Minor, where he converted the wife of a Roman proconsul. In retaliation the proconsul had Philip arrested and cruelly put to death.

MATTHEW the tax collector and writer of a Gospel, ministered in Persia and Ethiopia. Some of the oldest reports say he was not martyred, while others say he was stabbed to death in Ethiopia.

BARTHOLOMEW had widespread missionary travels attributed to him by tradition: to India with Thomas, back to Armenia, and also to Ethiopia and Southern Arabia. There are various accounts of how he met his death as a martyr for the gospel.

JAMES the son of Alpheus, is one of at least three James referred to in the New Testament. There is some confusion as to which is which, but this James is reckoned to have ministered in Syria. The Jewish historian Josephus reported that he was stoned and then clubbed to death.

SIMON, so the story goes, ministered in Persia and was killed after refusing to sacrifice to the sun god.

MATTHIAS was the apostle chosen to replace Judas. Tradition sends him to Syria with Andrew and to death by burning.

JOHN is the only one of the disciples thought to have died a natural death from old age. He was the leader of the church in the Ephesus area and is said to have taken care of Mary the mother of Jesus in his home. John was later exiled to the island of Patmos. There he is credited with writing the last book of the New Testament, Revelation. An early Latin tradition has him escaping unhurt after being cast into boiling oil at Rome.

Now, time for a few rhetorical questions. How were the disciples able to communicate with persons throughout the eastern hemisphere whom spoke different languages? How many of the Disciples were crucified or martyred for their belief and unwavering commitment to God's word and the teachings of Jesus Christ? Well, one more question. How many of the disciples became wealthy taking the money from their students and converts? Rhetorical because you should know the answer. How many great Christian evangelist or pastors or preachers or teachers today are executed or martyred? How many are millionaires? I know many are yelling, God blessed those men! I find it hard that God blesses them with the one thing that is the root of all evil.

After Jesus the two most influential apostles were Peter and Paul. Peter became one of Jesus' main guys. He spoke on Jesus behalf until his death. My point is Peter denied knowing Jesus. I guess Jesus knew the end from the beginning. Somehow, Jesus knew Peter's heart. If you do not understand my point, if you missed it or got it twisted, then go back or get the Bible. Too many people are impressed or swayed, by one's words. It is one's heart, we must discern. Another equally important apostle was Paul. We need to take note that Paul was originally Saul. He crucified Christians. And he has the most single influence on the Bible and the Church.

After the death of the apostles, faith continued to spread. In its own kind of way. But, remember at this time Christianity was still considered an illegal religion or belief. Actually, for centuries the original Christian teachings of Jesus were considered, blasphemy and outright forbidden. During the early years of Christianity disputes over the law caused great controversy. One of these laws was circumcision. Peter supported the idea of circumcision. Paul however made an argument that circumcision was not a necessary practice. Because Jesus taught that He came to "abolish" the LAW, Paul felt following certain laws would be contradiction to his doctrine of salvation through faith. Paul argued throughout his letters, that Gentiles should be accepted by God, without having to be circumcised. They could come to God without having to observe Kosher Laws! They could be forgiven of all their sins without having to enter the Temple once a year to slaughter an animal and spill its blood on the altar! From

Paul's perspective, the coming of Christ rendered that entire old form of the Jewish religion, redundant if not obsolete. Although competing forms of Christianity emerged early and persisted into the 5th century, there was a certain unity within the mainstream churches. What were those competing forms of Christianity? How was the religious beliefs unified? Who was the major player in causing this unification? First we will look at the first groups of Christians. Then we will discuss Constantine. We also will not forgot Europe, the monarchies, kings and bishops. Throughout time Christians become to exist and foster a particular love and dedication to the Trinity, they blossomed into wealth, became "Evangelical", capitalist and quite MAGAist.

The first Christians were the Jews who believed that Jesus was the Jewish messiah. They used an early Gospel of Matthew, and their beliefs were in accordance with the earliest reports of the gospels of Luke and Matthew, and with Jewish prophecy. Initially a sect of Judaism, Christianity first organized itself in Jerusalem. However, although Jewish Christianity was dominant at first, within twenty years it had moved out into the non- Jewish Gentile world.

Though they were never not considered an actual religious group the very first followers of Jesus were called the Nazoreans. This was a general name for the Jewish followers of Christ, but it is unknown to what extent they would be called Christians according to today's definition. They knew and understood many aspects of Jesus, both whom spoke Aramaic. Certain events led to the Nazoreans being dispersed and led to their demise. Many gentiles already called the Nazoreans Christians, but, we still know little about them. They ultimately disappeared. Why you should ask.

The second major group of Jesus followers were the Ebionites. The Ebionites were also some of the original Christians. They were mostly Jews who believed that Jesus was the Messiah and made up the original and legendary Jerusalem Church. 'Ebionite' was sometimes used as a term to describe all Christians. After discovering them and realizing that their beliefs differed, the

Pauline Christians were in opposition to the Ebionites. Many of the fanatical religious persons wrote against the Ebionites. It was not a coincidence that the Ebionites vowed to live in poverty. The Ebionites also adopted one of the first Christian documents, the Gospel of Matthew. All Christians were sometimes called Ebionites, although later Christians moved so far from their roots that they came to no longer recognize them. The Ebionites maintained their loyalty or commitment to claiming to be Jewish, with their major argument was Jesus was Jewish. Though other Christians disagreed, both Paul and James openly approved of their existence. Later Pauline Christians edited Gospels in order to dispute Ebionites beliefs and burnt all the Ebonite books. They arrested and abused the Ebionites until none were left.

In its earliest years, aside from the Nazoreans and Ebionites the Christian religion was divided into three major religious movements: the Gnostics, Jewish Christians, and Pauline Christians. Almost all current Christian groups trace their lineage back to the Pauline Christian movement. What was the Pauline Christians and how did it start?

The conflict between Paul and the Jerusalem apostles focused especially on whether Jews and Gentiles could eat together. According to Paul's account in Galatians, he had criticized Peter for withdrawing from eating meals with Gentiles after Jewish Christians had censured him for doing so. By including Gentiles in the church on an equal footing with Gentiles, Paul had laid the foundation for the separation of Christianity from Judaism.

Now, even when we view Paul as a pillar of Christian religion it may be shocking that, Paul did not convert to Christianity, nor did he view his ministry as founding a new religion. Paul always was, and always remained, a Jew who believed that his faith had reached its climax with the coming of Christ. The turning point in Paul's life was probably the blow up in Antioch over eating with gentiles. And from that point on, Paul works almost exclusively within gentile communities. Paul had strong beliefs pertaining to Adam, Eve and Abraham. He felt God promised

Abraham that 'all the families of the earth would be blessed. This was a promise that the entire world, Jew and Gentile alike would one day be included in God's family. No one would be excluded from this story of salvation. And Paul believed that the coming of Christ was the final chapter in this overarching story.

Paul thought that the whole meaning of Christ's coming was that all people, no matter who they were or what their background was, could approach God on the same equal playing field. As you might imagine, Paul made many enemies by advocating this new form of his ancient faith. He was labeled a 'liberal', a 'heretic', an 'anti-Jew', a friend of pagans. If today, we may call him a socialist. He was changing the symbols and practices of centuries of Jewish history. Paul wrote in Galatians, "there is 'no Jew or Gentile, slave or free, male or female, we are all one in Christ"

Now, why am I spending all this time writing about Paul? Because he felt all mistreated, poor, the abused and those shown injustice, lives should be forever lifted up, recognized and respected. The caveat is that not all Paul's followers were as humane and loving. They believed in inclusion but inhumane behavior. It is for this reason I personally believe the Ebionites were the more "Christian", holy and godly as oppose to the Pauline Christians who slaughtered, slandered and oppressed them. Unfortunately the victors get to write history, and it is Pauline Christianity that became the legacy of the Roman Empire. There was a struggle within going on in early Christianity that nearly ended Paul's entire ministry. It was a power struggle that would set Peter vs. Paul, and Paul vs. James. Please read about this read about this in Acts ch. 15, and Galatians ch. 2, Please.

When we look at early legitimate prophets, teachers and spiritual leaders, they all taught one thing. It is our duty, our obligation to teach others and strengthen our brothers and sisters in the ways of and intentions of God. Our heart should guide our intentions and our intentions should be humane and righteous. It is said over and over again' "do not be a false Prophet". Do not forsake God's children. There is again the parable where Jesus

Curses the fig tree. Observing a fruitless tree, Jesus curses it and it withers. Same as the disciples on the boat during the storm. Jesus wants us to have faith, bear good fruit, by encouraging others. Be an example, practice what we preach, teach what we have been taught. NOT sit under a pastor for ten, twenty, thirty years. Also do not entertain the false words of our government leaders. But, also bear good fruit. Be a witness and an example to the truth. But I am getting ahead of myself. So, Christianity still struggled to have a unique identity. The crucifixion of Jesus was to have an even more profound effect on the world to come.

Before I get into Rome let me mention Peter one more time. As stated earlier Peter was Jewish, but would posthumously transform his beliefs into one of the largest sects of Christians in history. The Gospels suggest Peter was the most prominent or even important apostle. This is in spite of the fact that he denied Jesus three times before the crucifixion. According to the scripture, Peter was the first disciple to whom Jesus appeared. Why do you think Jesus loved Peter and held him in high esteem? One reason was that Peter's faith and ultimate loyalty outweighed his denial. We see that throughout the Bible people are rewarded according to their faith, the heart and their ultimate sacrifice in doing what is right and just.

Peter wound up being the first leader of the early Church and if you remember, it was Peter's mother-in-law who was healed by Jesus. Peter is considered to be responsible for the start or founding of the Catholic church, though historians differ whether Peter was ever a Catholic. He was the first Bishop or predecessor to the first Pope. Ironically Peter was in Rome were he was ultimately crucified.

It wasn't until almost 300 years after the crucifixion of Jesus and the death of Peter and Paul that someone figured out a way to unify the Christian religion and make it a world-wide force. Someone figured out almost like a movie, how to bring the five families together and pay homage to the new Christian edict. It not only be noted, but should be understood with great reverence. All the groups previously mentioned were all abolished by imprisonment, slavery or death. The end to the true teaching of Jesus laid the foundation for the teaching and Christianity that the world would come to accept and embrace.

In AD 64, Emperor Nero, of Rome attempted to blame Christians for the Great Fire of Rome. It was during the reign of Nero that Peter and Paul were martyred in Rome. For the next two and a half centuries Christians suffered from various persecutions. Their refusal to participate in Imperial cult was considered an act of treason and was thus punishable by execution. During the Great Persecution (303–311), the emperor of Rome ordered Christian buildings and the homes of Christians torn down and their sacred books collected and burned. I recall Germany went through something like this over a thousand years later. Christians were arrested, tortured, burned, starved, and condemned to fight as gladiators to amuse spectators. The Great Persecution officially ended in April if the year 311.

The Roman Empire required Christians to worship the gods they deemed to be true. Christians' refusal to join pagan celebrations meant they were unable could not participate in much of public life. The Romans actually thought Christians were angering the gods and thereby threatening the peace and prosperity of the Empire. Christian became victims of persecutions. In spite of these persecutions, evangelization efforts persisted, leading to the Edict of Milan which legalized Christianity. What led to this turn around?

Around the year 250 BC a man was born named Constantius in the province of Dardania and the son of Eutropius, whom was a nobleman from northern Dardania. Yeah I never heard of it either! Constantius was a high ranking member under the emperor Aurelian and fought in the east against the secessionist Pamyrene Empire in Britain. He served as a roman soldier, and then a Roman officer before becoming emperor. His life story isn't that important, but his fling and son were. Constantius like many nobles was a philanderer, player type. After battles, he spent time in an inn where he met the innkeepers' daughter, Helena. They had a son Constantine, who was born about 272. Constantius made it to the high office in the Roman Empire in the west under Maximian. Throughout 287 and into 288, Constantius, under the command of Maximian, was involved in many wars against, carrying out attacks on the territory of the barbarian tribes across the Rhine and Danube rivers. To strengthen the ties between the emperor and his powerful military servant, in 289 Constantius divorced his wife (or concubine) Helena, and married the emperor Maximian's daughter, Theodora. By this time his son Constantine whom he cared for was proclaimed Caesar. Fourteen years later, Constantius died After Constanius death and after Constantine became emperor. Here is the part were Christianity takes a twist. A twist towards present day. Eighteen months later, Emperor Constantine made up for the neglect of his father to Helena, ordering all honor be paid to his mother. Constantine's mother Helena whom was a Christian, was granted much land around Rome. Helena was granted the title of Augusta by her son, and again she received financial rewards with the recognition.

Stories tell of Helena's travel to Palestine as an official of the construction of churches that Constantine had ordered. Stories also tell of Helena's role in the discovery of the True Cross, on which Jesus was crucified, finding the nails from the crucifixion and a tunic worn by Jesus before his crucifixion. In Jerusalem, she is credited with having a temple to Venus (or Jupiter) torn down and replaced with the Church of the Holy Sepulchre, where the cross was supposed to have been discovered. I repeat they were stories that were told. She also is reported to have ordered built a church on the location identified with the burning bush in the story of Moses.

Now this is a lot of history about Constantine's mother, but is necessary to understand what was about to happen. You see Constantine's mother was a Christian, his father an idolater. Helena was also labeled a Saint. After Constantine became the sole ruler of the Western Roman Empire, in honor of his mother, he issued the Edict of Milan in 313, which guaranteed religious tolerance for Christians. Emperor Constantine gave orders to build at Jerusalem an elaborate church in honor of the Resurrection of Christ Basically, it was claimed to have been built where Jesus was buried. The temple was constructed in about ten years. St. Helen did not survive to see the dedication of this temple. Now after supporting his mother, Constantine took edicts to a completely new level. In 323, when he became the sole ruler of the entire Roman Empire, he extended the provisions of the Edict of Milan to the Eastern half of the Empire. After three hundred years of persecution, Christians could finally practice their faith without fear. There was one caveat. All Christians must adopt and support the Nicean Creed. Why do you think this was important to Constantine? Constantine's mother was a Christian whom he loved dearly and had reached Saint like heights amongst the Romans. But his father was an idolater, who worshiped many gods. Out of love for his mother and loyalty to his father, he constituted the Nicean Creed.

This Creed would adopt the acceptance of three divine entities. All being equal as one.

Now there were several versions of the creed throughout about a one hundred year period. All were basically the same. In 431 The third Ecumenical Council not only reaffirmed the original 325 version of the Nicene Creed but declared that "it is unlawful for any man oppose the Nicene Creed verbally, or in writing of any form.

I was an acolyte in a Lutheran Church growing up and the Nicene Creed was recited every service. The Nicene Creed went something like this.

"We believe in one God, the Father, the Almighty, maker of heaven and earth, of all that is, seen and unseen. We believe in one Lord, Jesus Christ, the only Son of God, begotten son of the Father, God from God, Light from Light, true God from true God, begotten, not made, being one with the Father. Through him all things were made. He was born of the virgin Mary, crucified under Pontius Pilate; he suffered death and was buried. On the third day he rose again in accordance with the Scriptures; he ascended into heaven and is seated at the right hand of the Father. He will come again in glory to judge the quick and the dead, and his kingdom will have no end. We look for the resurrection of the dead, and the life of the world to come. Amen" Now this was the version I remember and I guess we recited it because though we were Lutheran, we were as close to Catholic as you could get. But it is the Creed from the mixing First Council of Nicea and the Council of Constantinople. The Council of Constantinople or Constantine added more including a part about believing in one holy catholic and apostolic Church Through the years this would play a key role and solidify Catholicism as the ruling religion of Europe as well as Protestant divisions with Catholic influence. And it was monumental in both the idea and the acceptance of the Trinity.

One thing to point out. The use of the word God in the Creed. Some may already know where I am going. Some are saying.." So what!!" Well one thing I myself would like to know what we called God back then. Again. The word God is a relatively new European inventive word, which was never used in any of the ancient Judaeo-Christian scripture manuscripts that were written in Hebrew, Aramaic, Greek or Latin. None of the prophets, worshippers or disciples who wrote various books of the Bible would even know or recognize or understand this word God. Yet we have spent centuries debating and more importantly fighting over it! So how did we get where we are today. Before we get to the meat and potatoes let's look at how Christianity morphed into whatever during the next many centuries.

The next thousand years or so, Christianity changed based on the views and divisions of the east and west Roman Empire. Since all of this would probably take volumes of books to explain, I will try to provide the short unabridged version. In short, in the east you had the monarchies, empires and emperors. In the west you had kings and the growth of the church, with the bishops and popes. For everyone that is thinking well the west should have been more Christian-like, keep reading. The emperors in Constantinople extended their reach to Italy, the British Isles, Germany and even North Africa. Though Africa was short lived do to Islam Good news. The church provided a sense of civility. The bishop of Constantinople were soon given equal status with the bishop of Rome. The church leaders, such as the popes began to move west, make pacts with the western secular leaders. As the popes teamed up with the "secular" rulers their influence grew in the east, as they anointed kings and themselves gained power. This ultimately resulted in a clear distinction between eastern and western Christianity. Throughout time the eastern Greek Orthodox developed and existed aside from the eastern Roman Catholic.

Moving along a few centuries. There was a distinct division between the Roman Catholic and Protestant religion. Mainly about the Trinity and the Nicene Creed. Though previously discussed and interesting reading, not pertinent for where I am heading.

As we get closer to Christianity in America, we must look at Medieval times, the Saxon Kingdoms and the rise of England as a power. As the growth and unions of the Saxon kingdoms grew, so did the power of the kings and lords. The so-called nobles were referred to with great reverence. Kings self- appointed themselves as "holy" and appointed by God. Some pastors today tell their congregation that God anointed them and personally place them at the head of the church and supplied their riches. The medieval kings hid under the false protection of the church. A church that was influenced by the fear of the kings as well as the riches it inherited. The west continued to extend the powers of the church, bishops and popes. By Medieval times the church would yield a lot of power. The Medieval church had power and control over the entire society. This included the land and the free labor from the peasants. The people were constantly threatened with the probability of Hell if not loyal. This loyalty included giving a minimum of ten percent tithes, weekly worship and joyful servitude. It was a cast system with three groups. lords, commoners and peasants. Pretty much how America kicked things off. The church in Medieval times made people pay for any service, even baptism. They used condemnation and fear to ensure payments to the church. Free from paying taxes... hmmm?! They accumulated a vast sum of money and soon had more wealth than any king during this period. As such, the church became wealthy. One of the wealthiest institutions on earth. One of the most important things that further defined society was the class system. This would be pertinent throughout Europe and affect the laws in the "new world" to come.

I do feel compelled to say that a lot of the practices of empires and the early church helped shape the inequality of man, the riches of empires and countries as well as some of the most heinous crimes in world history. From the Roman Empire to the Crusades, to the British Empire the church grew in influence and in the name of Christianity. Professed Christians played a key role in both the growth of Christianity as well as the growth of inequality.

Christianity should have been the foundation of society and culture. All empires and governments should have based their principles on Christianity. Instead, empires and culture shaped Christianity. With each new empire established after the death of Jesus, Christianity was changed. One should read more about the Roman, Byzantine, Ottoman and even England's empire. The role of Christianity and the church played an important role in early or Medieval Europe. The church mimicking Rome of the past ruled with power an injustice. They dominated the lives of the so-called commoner or peasants. Those peasants spent centuries as slaves called servants. They were the ones forced to pay the fictionally defines tithes to the church royalty. The great church sanctioned the pillaging and stealing of land. The role the church had on all these empires had a very profound effect on the founding of America. The foundation for religion in America was about to be established. As in all chapters I must unquestionably state, that there were good Christians, good men of God and good human beings throughout this time and all times.

Chapter Four

Christianity in Early America

hristianity in practice was prophesized in the Old Testament. Birthed in the New Testament. Shaped in the years after Christ. And now, would be a force and take the shape of what America would be in the future. For many readers the words will already be known and fully believed. For others they may find discourse and hold on to the beliefs passed down by their great grandparents. It is intended for the reader to understand how the country and actual religions formed as well as how they affected politics.

I would like to start out by saying I will focus on America after it was so-called newly discovered. Everyone should know that of over two million Native Americans inhabited Western World many of thousands of years before it was "colonized". There is also documentation to support the existence of Norseman, whom travelled west from Greenland. Erik the Red founded a settlement around the year 985 and his son Leif is believed to have spent time in what is now Canada. These facts are important because the truth should be a tenet of Christianity. But since our focus is who we are today I will move on to our American told history. We all know the story of Christopher Columbus. Who travelled by boat.. Nina, Pinta, Santa Maria… to the new World. Which again, happen to be occupied by millions of Native Americans. And was in no way done exclusively for Christian purposes. We will skip the fact it was an accident. The first so-called European colonist did not arrive on the soil of the New World for many years later. Is this relevant to the point? If you believe, the truth has anything to do with righteousness.

Many people were taught or just think that the first Europeans that came to America did so for religious freedom and other religious reasons. First let me state most of the people who came to America did so either for the chance at financial gain or as a refuge in an attempt to reinvent themselves. Those few who sought religious freedom did so for three reasons. One, they wanted to be able to choose between Catholicism and Protestant. Two, they wanted to adopt their own ritualistic interpretations of the Catholic or Protestant beliefs. Three, the church and government had too much power and influence on the day to day lives of its citizens. This was actually the main reason. In Europe, Catholic and Protestant nations often persecuted or forbade each other's religions, and British colonists frequently maintained restrictions against Catholics. Well, it was just like the old days. If the original colonist came to America for religious freedom, then Islam, Hinduism, Buddhism and all other religions would have flourished in America. Instead there was a price to pay if you were not a New World Christian. If you keep reading you will see our founding fathers actually tried to prevent the lack of religious freedom and the authoritative influence of the Christian church.

So, how many of the first settlers were Christians? The answer to this would depend on a few qualifications. One, do you consider the first settlers those who arrived with the first group of explorers, the settlers who arrived on the Mayflower, or those settlers in America after the Revolutionary War? If you are speaking about the Nina, Pinta, Santa Maria, none. If you are talking about the Mayflower, only around 100 pilgrims took the voyage. But, we could argue that America began during the first colonial establishments in the 17th century. Almost all Americans were taught that America was founded in the late 18th century with her break with Great Britain in the 1770s, and the creation of constitution in the 1780s and 1790s. A very serious caveat to the questions of the number of Christians, would also be, how many people professed to Christian. Or, how many thought they were Christian based on the warped evolution it became?

The role of religion in American has been a source of controversy since the nation's inception. Religious liberty and the relationship between church and state have always been and is still debated. Now let us spend just a few pages on how Christianity developed or grew in the colonies. We should know that Christianity was practiced long before the nation was founded and the Constitution adopted. Yes there was a religious movement that attached itself to the original colonies. But not as we are led to believe or was taught. Even though, many say those who wanted religious freedom founded America, there were only a small percentage of Christians. They would be the catalyst for many saved souls but also responsible for many early stake burnings, lynching, slavery and genocide. Blasphemous you say. Nah, just the truth.

Christianity was introduced to North America as it was colonized by Europeans, beginning in the 16th and 17th centuries. In the early years of America, there were still two main groups, Protestants and Catholics. We all know that within the Protestant group there were many denominations. But for all the denominations and sects, the United States was formed by followers and members of a very particular group. We will discuss after I bore you with how religion began in America. I will keep it brief as possible Northern European people introduced Protestantism to Massachusetts Bay Colony, New Netherland, Virginia colony, Carolina Colony, Newfoundland and Labrador, and Lower Canada. Among Protestants, there were practices of Methodism, the Baptist Church, Congregationalism, Presbyterianism, Lutheranism, Quakerism, Mennonite and Moravian Church.

The Spanish, French, and British brought Roman Catholicism to the colonies of New Spain, New France and Maryland respectively. Because the Spanish were the first Europeans to establish settlements on the mainland of North America, such as St. Augustine, Florida in 1565, the earliest Christians in the territory which would eventually become the United States were Roman Catholics. Jesuit settlers then introduced Catholicism to the English colonies in 1634, with the founding of the Province of Maryland. We will touch on all the divisions during the growth of the colonies.

The territory that would become the Thirteen Colonies in 1776 was largely populated by Protestants due to Protestant settlers seeking religious freedom from the Church. These settlers were primarily Puritans, whom we will discuss next. There were also some Anglicans and Catholics but these were far fewer in number. By the time of the American Revolution the English colonies became almost entirely Protestant. Many of the British North American colonies that eventually formed the United States of America were settled in the 17th century by men and women, who, refused to compromise their religious and suffered religious persecution, Thus during the Protestant Reformation which began around 1517 they fled Europe.

Now remember we are talked about the Pilgrims, but the Puritans, became a much larger group than the Pilgrims, established the Massachusetts Bay Colony in 1629 with four hundred settlers. It was also this early, that generationally wealthy companies sprouted. But, more on that later. The Puritans were the group whom disagreed with the Church of England and the Catholicism that the church represented. The Puritans were English Protestants called non-separatist whom were at odds with and wanted to change the Church of England. Many were seeking refuge from conflicts in England which led up to the English Civil War. Within two years, an additional two thousand Puritan settlers arrived. About twenty thousand Puritans migrated to America from England, beginning in the early 1600's, to gain the liberty to worship as they chose. Most settling in New England. The Puritans were thought to be a deeply religious group. Few doubt that Puritans were serious Christians. They were a tight-knit group socially and that is still present in the modern United States. Puritans hoped the New World would conform to the teachings of the Bible and become a nation whereby they could find redemption. Puritans separated church and state, but they clearly thought the two institutions should work in tandem to support, protect, and promote true Christianity.

The Puritans at that time were known to be true followers of Christianity and were unjustly ridiculed and even physically harmed. History however, tells us their righteousness took an ugly turn. I am sure everyone has heard of the Salem witch trials.

The Salem witch trials were a series of hearings before local magistrates followed by county court trials to prosecute people accused of witchcraft in Essex, Suffolk and Middlesex counties of colonial Massachusetts, between February 1692 and May 1693. Over one hundred and fifty people were arrested and imprisoned, with even more accused, but not formally pursued by the authorities. Now you would have to research each case, but I will say that many Puritans lost their minds. I will even say they lost sight of the teachings of Jesus. I should mention that the burning at the stake was a European practice and popularized later by movies. The Puritans actually began committing the same acts of persecution as they supposedly fled from in Europe. Two Salem courts convicted twenty-nine people of the capital felony of witchcraft. Nineteen of the accused, fourteen women and five men, were hung. One man, Giles Corey, who refused to enter a plea was crushed to death under heavy stones in an attempt to force him to do so. At least five more of the accused died in prison. Even though, the Puritans were English Protestants, who sought to purify the Church of England of Roman Catholic practices, they followed Medieval old Holy Roman Empire's laws that said witchcraft should be punished by fire. This is similar to some of today's Christian beliefs and practices that serve the leaders of certain political and religious groups. The Puritans would all but disappear but the practice of unjust persecution for various differences would flourish. So what religious group would ensure the nation actually would be something Jesus taught? That may be answered in another book. Since there was no state religion, in fact there was not yet a state, and there was no centrally controlled authority, religious practice in the colonies became very diverse.

The Quakers who were originally the Religious Society of Friends formed in England in 1652 around leader George Fox. Although the Quakers may have resembled the Puritans in some religious beliefs and practices, they differed with them over the necessity of compelling religious uniformity in society. They also differed in their insane persecutory rituals. In 1681, Quaker leader William Penn parlayed a debt owed by Charles II to his father into a charter for the Province of Pennsylvania. Quakers were already prepared to grasp the opportunity to live in a land where they might worship freely. By 1685, as many as eight thousand Quakers had come to Pennsylvania and Delaware. At this point in our history I would say the Quakers belief system, simple ways and ridicule, represented the closest practice of Christianity.

Martin Luther founded Lutheranism, a Protestant religious denomination, during the 1500s when he was excommunicated from the Catholic Church. He originally intended only to reform Roman Catholicism, but he formed his own religious faith. Lutherans formed regional and national denominations based on geography, ethnicity, and theological differences. Delaware was originally settled by Lutherans of New Sweden. In 2015 there were close to seven million Lutherans in America.

As earlier stated, the Spanish conquistadors brought Catholicism to settlers in Florida just before the Protestant Reformation in 1517. Roman Catholicism is the largest of the three major branches of Christianity. We must understand that all Roman Catholics are Christian, but not all Christians are Roman Catholic. The first Christian worship service held in the current United States was supposedly a Catholic Mass in Pensacola, Florida. Maryland was one of the few regions among the English colonies in North America that was predominantly Catholic. The

Maryland Toleration Act, issued in 1649, which defines religious tolerance was considered a precursor to the First Amendment. Well as long as it was Christian. Until the American Revolution, Roman Catholics in Maryland were considered outcast while keeping loyal to their convictions. Catholicism went through many changes. At the time of the Revolution, Roman Catholics formed less than one percent of the population of the thirteen colonies, in 2007, Roman Catholics comprised twenty four percent of US population.

The Church of England was legally established in the Colony of Virginia in 1619. This meant that local taxes could be funneled through the local parish to handle the needs of local government, such as roads and poor relief, in addition to the salary of the minister. There never was a bishop in colonial Virginia, and in practice the local vestry consisted of laymen controlled the parish.

The first churches in the new world mimicked those in England where the parish became a unit of local importance. A parish was a group of churches organized in a way to provide each with financial support. This practice would be the catalyst for many practices today. The leader of the parish was known as a rector. It was governed by a respected of members known as the vestry. There were several problems with these religious units. First the congregation were not really devout in their attentiveness and behavior. Second, there were not enough pastors to meet the needs of the vast population. Third, ministers encouraged the congregation to basically adopt home Bible study and worship. This ultimately which pulled people away from the established church and fueled the First Great Awakening. It also necessitated that the church gain or regain its influence, which it did for centuries to come. In short, our take away from all the previous religious overview is that the early church structure laid the groundwork for today's denominational structure. The church whether Protestant or Catholic grew in influence, power and wealth. The evangelical era grew later in the twentieth century. They took a very elitist approach and produced many millionaires.

Early colonial laws and constitutions such as the Mayflower Compact, the Fundamental Orders of Connecticut, and Massachusetts Body of Liberties contain language incorporated from biblical texts. Through time this would change. The Charter of Liberties and Frame of Government of the Province of Pennsylvania (1681) begins by making it clear that God has ordained government, and it even quotes Romans 13 to this effect. Article 38 of the document lists "offenses against God" that may be punished by the magistrate, including, swearing, cursing, lying, profane talking, drunkenness, obscene words, incest, sodomy, cards, and dice. They felt these things and the like, excited the people to rudeness, cruelty and looseness. And once again this would drastically change in the years to come. We all know that today, lying is defended and seemingly honored and respected by many. As time went on at least nine of the 13 colonies had established churches, and all required officeholders to be Christians. They expected officeholders to be the committed confession type Christian. Not so much as far as behavior or morals. If one is to understand the story of the United States of America, it is important to have a proper appreciation for its Christian colonial roots. Most of the colonists of European descent who settled in the New World were professed Christians whose constitutions, laws, and practices reflected the influence of Christianity. Just the influence. No matter when we think this country was formed, how many Christians came to America or the validity of the first churches, our religious enthusiasm would take a very negative turn.

Now let us specifically look at a few of our Founding Fathers. There are different views and teachings as to whom were the Founding Fathers. Some think they were those men who signed the Declaration of Independence, but would not include George Washington, John Jay, Alexander Hamilton, and James Madison. Not to confuse there were also those men referred to as the "Framers" who took part in drafting the proposed Constitution. I will focus on the most known of the two groups. Before I start you should make note that many Evangelical speakers and pastors will claim the Founding Fathers were born again Christians. But this is not quite true. Let me explain what I mean from a religious perspective.

The Founding Fathers have been historically classified in terms of two religious groups. Protestant and Deist. A few were considered to be atheist, but that isn't a religion. Most of the Founding Fathers identified as being Protestant and did the basic church thing. Meaning they were a denomination of Christianity other than Catholicism. When we dive into the religious beliefs of Protestants we need to understand what were the different views and the founding fathers whom held different views. Where we begin to see the founding of our country separate from Christian philosophy widens with the introduction of Deism. Catholicism was not a factor until way in the twentieth century. Of course it was not a factor in America. The distinctions of philosophies among the Founding Fathers began with the Protestants and those who identified as being Deist. Deism has been explained many different ways. From an academia perspective, a layman's and a New World Christian perspective.

So there were founders whom were Christian and they retained a religious view. They believed in the sanctity of the Bible, divinity of Jesus Christ, and adhered to teachings of their particular denomination or church beliefs. Though, I am using the term sanctity very, very loosely. There were those who were sort of half Christian. They practiced Christian rituals or behaviors but were influenced by Deism. Last but not least, there were those who were Deist.. These divisions in religious philosophy were sort like divisions among our political parties. By that I actually mean political parties were formed by the early politicians taking sides on their religious views. Deism changed the views of orthodox Christians or Protestants. Quickly speaking Deism grew out of Europe's Age of Enlightment during the 1700 and 1800's. The Age of Enlightenment came from a group of scientific, mathematical and philosophical thinkers. They believed that everything in the universe could be rationalized, explained and demystified.

Deism, looked to the natural world for answers about God, life, death and spirituality. Those who were influenced by this age believed God made the universe but did not cause any physical phenomena. This age produced people like Iassac Newton, Galileo and Benjamin Franklin. Those influenced by Deism were not committed to reading the Bible, or really even praying. They did not believe in the need to attend church, to be baptized, or take Holy Communion. Another fact about Deist, they did not use the distinctions of God or Jesus Christ. Instead they used terms such as Creator, Almighty, Great One, etc. A Deist is one who believes in the existence of a God or supreme being but denies revealed religion, basing his or her belief on the light of nature and reason. Deists reject the Judeo-Christian accounts of God as well as the coloring book stories or apologues of the Bible. They do believe that God is eternal and good, but flatly reject having a relationship with Him through Christ. In today's society, Deist would be similar to those confessing 'Spirituality'. Some Founding Fathers were Deist, some Christian. Many of these founders feared what would happen if America mimicked the religious characteristics of the Old World. Did this affect how the country was founded and did it influence religion in America? Let us take a look.

Newly elected as first President of the United States, George Washington was born in 1732 in Westmoreland County, Virginia. He was born into a somewhat privileged family with two older half-brothers. His father was a leading plantation owner and a justice of the county court. When his father died, he gained control of the family business as well as slaves. Washington inherited ten slaves as a youth and went on to own over five hundred. We may all know he was a general but we may not know he was one of only nine Presidents who never went to college. Hopefully, we all know that George Washington did not have wooden teeth nor did he chop down a cherry tree. In 1755 at the early age of 23, Washington was made commander of all Virginia troops.

Now the most important part. What were his political, religious and social views? George Washington's great-grandfather and his father were vestrymen for their parishes in Virginia. This caused him to be nurtured in a church environment. But during the course of his life he grew apart from the traditional Christian behaviors and adopted a more Deist way of thinking. I will save this tidbit for later, for each Founding Father whom were influenced by Deism or Orthodox Christianity shared common philosophies on how the country should be formed.

As many of the Founding Fathers, Washington did not support the colonist idea of revolting against Britain. After several restrictions and taxes levied against the colonist Washington changed his mind. This is an important factor in the cause of the colonies to seek independence. We will discuss more about that later. In 1775 after the battle of Lexington and Concord Washington was appointed General and Commander in Chief of the colonial army against Britain. Everyone knows the rest. Washington's army defeated the British and he became the first President of the United States.

As President, he would have many political, social and religious quandaries. During his inaugural speech, he did ask for God's hand to bless the new republic and continued favor on our nation. Washington prayed that the Almighty Being bless the people of the United States with all due liberties and happiness. However, he believed that God's focus and blessing were for the benefit and protection of men not a country or government. He also believed if the country was men and woman of God, then the country would have to be blessed by default. This thinking was a factor in the forming of our nation. Throughout his prayer he never said God. But used terms as Almighty Being, Great Author, the Ruler of great events and the Invisible Hand. Washington's viewpoint on the government was that the country should not rely on any specific religious belief based on the Bible but on the inherent righteousness of its citizens. As he grew as a man and a person, he believed in the equality for all. It would be short-sighted of me not to mention that Washington gave freedom to his slaves in his will. In his will, written several months before his death in December 1799, George Washington left directions for the emancipation of all the slaves that he owned, after the death of Martha Washington. Do you know why?

Last but not least. In February of 1777 Washington issued the order to have all troops inoculated and ordered all recruits arriving in Philadelphia be inoculated. Hopefully everyone can see the correlation. Very important note.

Another well-known founding father was John Adams. The first Vice- President and the second President of the United States also had his idea of how religion should be considered in the framing of the new government. John Adams was born in 1735 in Massachusetts. His father was a deacon and his mother came from a well-known and respected medical family. As well as being President, he was an attorney, diplomat and writer. Like his predecessor he served a critical role in the fight for separation from British rule. Adams began his career very conservative and did not think the colonist should talk about taking up arms. As Britain's discretions mounted Adams soon changed his mind and help drafted a resolution adopted by the House of Representatives threatening independence as an alternative to tyranny. As far as his religion, he was raised in a Protestant environment but later his views of religion changed and he identified with Unitarianism. What is Unitarianism you may ask? It is another form of Deism. Like other Deist Adams did not follow or believe traditional Christian doctrine, such as the Trinity and the divinity of Jesus. However, he was certainly open to the teachings of Christ, though most accept all religions as valid expressions of faith. Actually a few religions but one major one, believe in and accept the teachings of Jesus. He felt that religion should not be a part of the principle foundation of the government. Adams felt it would be the best of all possible worlds, if there were no religion in it at all. At that time he also did not believe that no individual was totally depraved. Like many people today. During Adam's administration the Senate ratified the 1797 Treaty of Peace and Friendship with Tripoli, which states in Article XI that "the government of the United States of America is not in any sense founded on the Christian Religion." That said, he never owned slaves.

Another founding father Benjamin Franklin was born on January 17, 1706, in Boston, Massachusetts. His father's side of the family were born in England and his mother's side in Massachusetts. Franklin was a politician, writer, orator and inventor. We all know the stories of him discovering electricity by flying a kite. Benjamin Franklin. Did you also know he also invented bifocals, the lightning rod, swim fins and the urinary catheter? He was also quite a word-smith coining phrases like, don't throw stones at your neighbors, if your own windows are glass and haste makes waste. Franklin was a thinker and a philosophizer which heavily influenced his spiritual beliefs. He used all his knowledge and education to do his to make wise decisions when it came to the founding of our country. He was also a slave owner.

Franklin believed in God but described himself as a Deist. Like his counter parts he believed God governs the affairs of men, not countries. He felt the least we should do to honor God is respect His creation and do good unto all His children. It was up to the individual to do the right thing. If each citizen lived and honored God then the country would follow suit. He did have enough biblical knowledge to understand that without God's assistance with governing the hearts of men, the country would be built, just as the tower of Babel. Did he have a crystal ball?

Franklin also stated that though he respected and honored Jesus Christ, His teachings have been corrupted and therefore no place in government. Franklin's view on Christianity reflected many of the Founding Fathers.

Let us look at Patrick Henry. Best known for his "give me liberty or give me death" speech on March 23, 1775 Henry was born in 1736 in Hanover County, Virginia. Now Patrick Henry was a professed Christian though many of his political views were similar to Deist. Here is a verified quotation from a letter to his daughter dated August 20, 1796: "Amongst other strange things said of me, I hear it is said by the deists that I am one of the number; and indeed, that some good people think I am no Christian. This thought gives me much more pain than the appellation of Tory; because I think religion of infinitely higher importance than politics; and I find much cause to reproach myself that I have lived so long, and have given no decided and public proofs of my being a Christian. But, indeed, my dear child, this is a character which I prize far above all this world has, or can boast."

And in his will: "This is all the inheritance I give to my dear family. The religion of Christ will give them one which will make them rich indeed". See I am trying to be objective. Was he talking about spiritual or economic riches? Patrick Henry was the first to argue for the state to legislate and budget for the high salaries to those who chose the ministry. Henry's 1784 proposal wanted to provide state funds to a variety of churches. One opponents of Henry's plan was James Madison. Again, a mixed bag.

James Madison the fourth US President was born in 1751 on a plantation in Virginia. James Madison was the oldest of twelve children. His father was a tobacco planter who grew up on a five thousand acre plantation, then called Mount Pleasant, which he had inherited upon reaching adulthood. Madison's father was the largest landowner and a leading citizen in the Piedmont. Madison's maternal grandfather was a prominent planter and tobacco merchant. Their family owned an estimated one hundred slaves. The fact he had slaves will be visited later. And, probably not for the reasons you may think. Madison was a political leader, mathematician, diplomat and philosopher. He also studied the Enlightment. So I guess you know he was a Deist. He was also played a key role in writing or collaborating on the Constitution of the United States and the United States Bill of Rights.

Back to Patrick Henry's vision to have the states fund the churches. James Madison disagreed and felt that "the Holy Author of our Religion" did not require state support. He also felt as many politicians at that time that Christianity was far purer before "Constantine first established Christianity by human Laws." But Madison's argument was rejected and supporters believed that support was necessary to attract good God fearing candidates to the ministry. The Founders who stood on the Christian value argument were committed to the idea that Christian religion was necessary for public happiness and political prosperity. In the long run, was this a good thing.

Now let us look at Thomas Jefferson. Thomas Jefferson was born in 1743 on a plantation in Virginia. A wealthy landholder, he had owned about six hundred slaves who served in his household and on his plantations. Thomas Jefferson was the main writer of the Declaration of Independence. In his initial draft of the Declaration of Independence, Thomas Jefferson. Jefferson thus acknowledged that slavery violated the natural rights of the enslaved, while at the same time he absolved Americans of any responsibility for owning slaves themselves. In 1802, Thomas Jefferson wrote a letter to the Danbury Baptist Association in which he suggested that the First Amendment created a "wall of separation between Church & State." He believed that religion was a matter which lied solely between Man and his God. He also felt that no man should have to account to another for his faith or his worship. Finally, he declared that their legislature should "make no law respecting an establishment of religion, or prohibiting the free exercise thereof". This was the building a wall of separation between Church and State. Jefferson did however seem somewhat conflicted at times. As governor he did draft a bill stipulating the governor could appoint days of public fasting and thanksgiving and even humiliate and punish "Disturbers of Religious Worship and Sabbath Breakers. As a member of the Continental Congress, he proposed that the nation adopt a seal containing the image of Moses extending his hand over the sea, overwhelming the Pharaoh, and the motto "Rebellion to tyrants is obedience to God. I do question his narrow definition of tyrant. Jefferson closed his second inaugural address by requesting all

Americans take his lead and ask for "the favor of that Being in whose hands we are, who led our forefathers, as Israel of old…." Yes somewhat spiritual, but not necessarily Christian. Notice his use of the term, "that Being" Even though Jefferson favored a stricter separation between church and state than virtually any other founder he did not attempt to completely remove religion from the public life. Ironically his opinion of Christianity can be brought to our attention by these words he spoke. This from Thomas Jefferson in an April 11, 1823, letter to John Adams: "The day will come when the mystical generation of Jesus by the Supreme Being in the womb of a virgin, will be classed as a fable But we may hope that the dawn of reason and freedom of thought in these United States will do away with all this artificial scaffolding " While Thomas Jefferson was the genius behind the Declaration of Independence, John Jay, Alexander Hamilton and James Madison were the brains providing the intellectual foundation of our Constitution.

John Jay had a somewhat conflicting history. He was born into a wealthy family of merchants and New York City government officials. And though he successfully passed gradual emancipation legislation as governor of New York, and was the founder of the Manumission Society (basically advocating against slavery), he owned at least six slaves. History tells us that he continued to purchase enslaved people in order to emancipate them once he considered their work resulted in just cause. He was also influenced by concerns about the growth of the black population within the United States and the 'degradation' of blacks under slavery. John Jay was a Christian and held offices in many Christian Societies. He did however feel that Christians should not provoke war and abstain from violating the rights of others. His main point was that since most nations had rulers whom were not elected, America should elect Christian officials therefore minimizing the decisions to go to war. He also expressed a belief that the moral precepts of Christianity were necessary for good government and society needed to have the moral precepts of the Christian Religion to maintain peace and equality. John Jay knew that without that basic philosophy of decency our country would be doomed. Well I guess he was right.

Alexander Hamilton came from a more humble background and is known for his historic death. Remember Aaron Burr and the infamous duel. It is told that Hamilton used religion for political ends. He called Jefferson "the atheist," and said that Christianity and Jefferson's view on democracy were mutually exclusive. He may have taken pictures in front of a church holding a bible. After 1801, Hamilton further attested his belief in Christianity, proposing a Christian Constitutional Society in 1802 to take hold of "some strong feeling of the mind" to elect "fit men" to office, and advocating "Christian welfare societies" for the poor. After being shot, Hamilton spoke of his belief in God's mercy.

I wrote of a select few to point out throughout history leaders differed in their opinions of the role religion should play in society. America's Founders did not want Congress to establish a national church, like that of England. Many also opposed establishments at the state level as well. Yet they believed, as George Washington declared in his Farewell Address, that of "all the dispositions and habits which lead to political prosperity, religion and morality are indispensable supports". I understand the political reason why they made sure religion was not incorporated into the Constitution or influenced by government. They knew if the government gave people their freedom and subtlety encouraged Christianity they would have a peaceful, productive and caring citizen. They also were well read students of history and knew how religion led to the downfall of just about every prior nation. There were however many religious symbols and scriptures carved in stone which were important to the plan of the founding fathers of this nation prospering for centuries.

Okay, it is also evident our nation's Founders were not all Christian. And even if we can say, that a particular Founder was a member, regular attendee, and even officer in a church, it does not necessarily mean he was a sincere Christian. We know that many of them were Deist. I will say that many were spiritual.

They believed in God. Another possibility is that many of the Founders acted as Christians in their private and/or public lives. Some historians have argued that the Founding Fathers cannot be called Christian because some of them did not join churches, take communion, or remain faithful to their spouses. I would disagree for two reasons. First, which many may disagree, church does not make or justify a Christian. We were called to start churches not be life-long members. Second, because many were 18th century Christians. What do I mean by that? During the course of history, Christianity changed. The disciples, the Romans, the Saxons, the British and the Americans. Were they all Christians as Jesus intended? Half my readers may say yes. The other half may say no. Well then there are those that would say, they couldn't care less. Some would say they were not Christian because they either owned or condoned slavery. They did not act in a Christian manner if judged by the Fruits of the Spirit. They instituted a class system, did not abolish slavery and did not use the church in the manner the Bible teaches. They used war to take land from Indians and Mexicans.

To take a contemporary example, one should be very careful in saying, for instance, that someone is a good Christian politician only if he or she votes for (or against) tax cuts or national health care. Or others may say a good Christian would be anti-abortion. I would say a Christian politician or any one from any spiritual religion, would be in favor of all things right and righteous. They would as well oppose all things unrighteous, based on spiritual scripture. Not a political doctrine, dictator, base or president. It's that simple.

What we can definitely conclude is that the founding fathers were influenced by Christian ideas. But also, influence by their negative opinions of Christianity and their heartbreaking observations of Christians and Christian run governments. So, I will say emphatically that Christianity had a profound influence on the Founders. So is this good or bad? The Deist Founding Fathers did not oppose a Christian government because they had disdain for Christ or loved Satan. I say again, they opposed Christianity because they saw what it had done to their native country as well as other nations throughout history. All of them believed that a person's inherent rights come from God, not government and it is a personal relationship. They also believed that governments should be formed to protect one's rights. As we know this philosophy did not include all men and is still twisted. Before proceeding, I should emphasize that I am not arguing that Christianity was the only significant influence on America's Founders or that it influenced each Founder in the exact same manner. Clearly, Deism had very different, but often overlapping, intellectual influences in the era. All the Founders were also influenced, by the Anglo–American political–legal tradition and their own political experience, and like all humans, they were motivated to varying degrees by self, class, or state interests. We also must understand the Founding Fathers had two main goals in mind. One, to lay the foundation for a new nation, unlike any other, that guaranteed its citizens, or most, the right to seek prosperity. Two, to ensure the foundation they laid would prosper for centuries to come. The lack of the right of all living in the country to be named the United States, to prosperity and equality is probably my biggest pet peeve with the Christian debate. The founding fathers were intelligent and well read. They all knew the past fate of nations governed by the church and religion. My contention is merely that Christianity may have had an insignificant influence on America's Founders but this influence turned out to be a very significant event.

Many reading may have thought I was going down a road which would end in me saying that America turned out the way it did because many of the Founding Fathers were Christian. Some may have thought I was going to say America is in its current predicament because many of the founding fathers were not Christian. Food for thought. It was actually a combination. A combination that led to division, pride and broken country, out of the gate. Many had already been tainted with the perverted and twisted teachings of Jesus throughout the centuries. Most of the professed, zealous Christians leaders were from the south. Most of the Diest and spiritual leaders were from the North. The difference in religious and spiritual views actually led to the varied political and religious opinions. It also set the stage for the growth of denominations and the conservative Christians standing firm on their belief that their blessings emboldened them to protect their economic and social views. So, what am I saying is, keep reading.

Now we can look at the documents or declarations that spelled out the purpose and solidified who we were as a nation. A few documents that were the foundation for our eco-socio-political system. The facts of our history are easy enough to verify. Anybody who insists that our nation was founded on Christian ideals should understand the intent of the Founding Fathers and then need only look at the most important documents from our early history. The Federalist Papers, the Declaration of Independence, and the Constitution and the Bill of Rights.

The three main documents, the Declaration, Constitution and Bill of Rights share some similarities. Besides having preambles, they were all drafted by like men of similar backgrounds, financial status and color. The Declaration, the Constitution, and the Bill of Rights are all based on the idea that all people have certain fundamental rights. Rights to freedom and equality. One important right is the insurance that the government will protect those rights. The Founders believed that these natural rights were inherent in all people given by God and should never be surrendered to government. The drafters of the Declaration of Independence did so to express their desire to break away from the British government. The same framers drafted the Constitution and Bill of Rights in order to establish a government.

The Declaration of Independence, the most famous document produced by the Continental Congress during the War for Independence. The Declaration of Independence made certain sort of assertions and yapped about fundamental and inherent liberties. But if we think about it those liberties didn't become legally enforceable until they were written, set forth and ratified in the Constitution and the Bill of Rights .I would like to point out the Declaration of Independence was wholly written to declare the specific reasons why the colonies wanted to be independent from Europe. What were those reasons? As mentioned I would come back to this. First let me write about the cause of the Revolutionary War.

The Founding Fathers had several gripes with Britain. Depending on whom you obtained your knowledge from the cause of these gripes may vary. There are two main views on the cause of the war. One is taxes. The other is religious freedom. There were actually a few more things, the Founding Fathers, as well as the colonist objected. Let me discuss those right quick before I tackle the religious freedom case.

A little backstory. Britain has several so-called colonies throughout the world. The two most known were the West Indies and India. Those colonies along with America enjoyed a relative peaceful and successful existence. In 1760, King George the Third took the throne. During his reign, he and his ministers implemented quite a few changes from the previous monarchy. Prior to his rule, the colonist enjoyed certain freedoms very much like the other global colonies. But with George III rule things changed. First there were a few Acts imposed on the colonist.

The Sugar Act. Britain passed the first law to tax the revenue from colonies in order to raise money for the Crown. The act increased duties on non-British goods shipped to the colonies. desiring,

The Stamp Act was Britain's first direct tax on the colonies. Like the Sugar Act this was imposed to raise money for Britain. It taxed various goods such as a wide range of publications, legal documents, and many gambling products such as dice and cards.

Currency Act. This act imposed regulation whereby the colonist had to use Britain currency, prohibiting American colonies from issuing their own currency.

Quartering Act. Required the colonies to provide barracks and supplies to British troops.

Besides from these acts the British parliament imposed other new laws that infuriated the colonist. One, colonist were not allowed to vote or be represented in the British Parliament. This truly supported their chants of "No taxation without Representation". Kind of hypocritical! Another law imposed was an act limiting and in some cases prohibiting immigration to any British colony in America. There was also tariffs placed on tradeable goods to India, Ireland and the West Indies. King George imposed all of these sanctions which infuriated the colonist and Founding Fathers whom previously opposed any protest or separation.

Beginnings of Colonial Opposition. American colonists responded to the Sugar Act and the Currency Act with protest. In Massachusetts, participants in a town meeting cried out against taxation without proper representation in Parliament, and suggested some form of united protest throughout the colonies. By the end of the year, many colonies were practicing nonimportation, a refusal to use imported English goods. So in short, the Revolutionary War was not fought so colonist could practice Christianity but it was more about the money. That is my blurb about the religious reasons.

Following the Revolutionary War, the Declaration of Independence was formally signed. The document solidified our separation from England and the founding of America as an autonomous nation. The declaration proclaims, "We hold these truths to be self-evident: that all men are created equal; that they are endowed by their Creator with certain unalienable rights; that among these are life, liberty and the pursuit of happiness." Was the statement about equality and the pursuit of happiness, derived from a sense of humanity and equality? Or was it a political sound bite? Who is the Creator referenced in the document? Why is the term Creator used? Everyone should know the answer to that question. Now it can be surmised that at that time the authors of the Declaration of Independence were only referencing those who came from Europe. Not Native Americans, nor Asians and certainly not slaves. Nothing in that statement came to pass for many slaves, immigrants and poor citizens. Nothing in that statement comes close to living up to what the God or the Creator intended. Christians did not stand up and oppose oppression. Instead, many agreed to go the war to continue the right to oppress a people. Note that the framers of this document ensured all federal power was derived by the government or the people and figuratively not from God. In no case are any powers given to religion in the affairs of man. Man was supposed to practice what they preached. So on the very first day of our countries history we started out letting a particular group of men set the stage for things to come.

The Federal Papers were a collection of essays written and dispersed to the colonist to promote the ratification of the United States Constitution. James Madison wrote in his Federalist Papers, "If men were angels, no government would be necessary. If angels were to govern men, neither external or internal controls on government would be necessary." This conviction led them to adopt a constitutional system characterized by separated powers, checks and balances, and federalism. However this may have turned out, it was actually done with good intentions. Many Enlightenment thinkers in this era, by way of contrast, tended to favor a strong, centralized government run by experts.

The Constitution is a document that was written to establish a government after the United States was independent. It is divided into Articles. As with the Federalist Papers at no time does the Constitution mention "God" or faith in any of its many paragraphs. The U.S. Constitution is a wholly secular document. It contains no mention of Christianity or Jesus Christ. Article VI, prohibits "religious tests" for public office. So how did our government ensure that no one who professed any other religion ever became President? And though the constitution forbids "religious test" it is a known fact that a candidates religion should not affect his or her popularity. But we all know it does. We will discuss more about the amendments when we discuss the Bill of Rights.

Religion is only discussed in the context of keeping matters of faith separate from concerns of governance, and of keeping religion free from government interference. The founding fathers could not be clearer on this point. God has no role in government. Christianity has no role in government. So why would certain government officials and citizens quote anything in the Constitution as their argument and badge of Christianity. They make this point explicitly, repeatedly, in multiple founding documents. James Madison, in his first significant public act, objected to the use of "toleration" in the article, believing that it implied that religious liberty was a grant from the state that could be revoked at will. The Virginia Convention agreed, and the final draft of Article XVI was reprinted and by the end of the Revolutionary era, every state offered significant protection of religious liberty. Article XVI of the Constitution was amended to make it clear that "the free exercise of religion" is a right, not a privilege granted by the state.

The Constitution states: We the People, to form a more perfect Union, establish Justice, insure domestic Tranquility, provide for the common defense, promote the general Welfare, and secure the Blessings of Liberty to ourselves and our Posterity...." At the convention of National Reform Association, there was an attempt to replace part of the preamble that said, "We the People of the United States, in Order to form a more perfect Union" with, "Recognizing Almighty God as the source of all authority and power in civil government, and acknowledging the Lord Jesus Christ as the governor among the nations, his revealed will as the supreme law of the land, in order to constitute a Christian government " Of course this never happened. If it had, would it have made a difference. One may think that is where I am going. But, it would have probably been worse. Even more hypocritical and much more disrespectful in God's eyes.

Last but not least the Bill of Rights. The Constitution has been amended twenty-seven times, or somewhere around there. An amendment is a change or correction made to the Articles. It really should be an improvement. The first ten amendments to the Constitution are called the Bill of Rights even though the name is somewhat nebulous. They were supposedly inspired by Thomas Jefferson, definitely drafted by James Madison and were ratified in 1791. The last amendment was ratified in 1992. We all know the most regurgitated amendments. The First Amendment is freedom of religion, speech, assembly and the right to petition the government. All these can be questioned, if you have not lived in a bunker for the past 100 years. The Amendment actually states, "Congress shall make no law respecting an establishment of religion, or prohibiting the free exercise thereof; or abridging the freedom of speech, or of the press; or the right of the people peaceably to assemble, and to petition the Government for a redress of grievances. In the face of popular outcry, the first Congress proposed and the states ratified a constitutional amendment prohibiting Congress from restricting the free exercise of religion. What evolved were a multitude of military service exclusions, taken advantage of by many persons including Presidents. But at a minimum, it prohibits Congress from compelling "men to worship God in any manner contrary to their conscience." This also contributed to today's situation. The right to assemble is enforced unless you are a certain minority or the President wants to take a picture with a Bible. As I previous said the Constitution basically established the laws to back up the Declaration of Independence. But, as we see a lot of our laws are subjective, can be twisted and randomly apply. The Second Amendment is one that just racks my brain. The right to bear arms. Assault rifles, fifty caliber, automatic whatever. At this point in our history it is the most argued and defensible amendment. It is what many Christians use to make their bed. However, the entire amendment reads as follows, "A well regulated Militia being necessary to the security of a free State, the right of the people to keep and bear Arms shall not be infringed". I will not get into a debate about the comprehension of simple English. Everyone comprehends this in his or her own logical or twisted way. This amendment as we know will result in serious consequences. Christian nation or not.

Now let's discuss the Civil War. I ask everyone who flies, flaunts and freely waves the Confederate flag, or those historians who think they may know the answer. Why did the South decide to take up arms against the United States of America? There is a catch. In your answer you have to use either God or Jesus and back it up with truth. If you feel God wanted you to excel economically on the backs, sweat and death of God's children you need to either start over of give up. You must use the Bible, in its entirety. Show that you did not read two scriptures but the entire book, with full understanding. You cannot use the Constitution. I repeatedly hear the phrase, "to protect our way of life". I humbly ask, what was that way of life? Was it a Christian way of life? What happened over a hundred years ago, soiled our country for years to come. I really took time to look at this objectively and come up with a Christian reason for the thought process and actions of the Confederacy. I cannot. I can only read comments and letters. I could only listen to the stories told to me by relatives. I can only recall how I was treated when I went to North Carolina in the sixties. Imagine one hundred years earlier. I definitely did not hear any pleasantries, niceties or comforting retorts. So lets try to unravel the Christian motivation behind the Confederacy's point of view.

The Civil War according to the history taught in school started because a group of southern states disagreed with the Federal government mandates that would lead to the abolishment of the southern economic and cultural freedoms. I asked two teachers what this meant. One said, "the north wanted to limit the economic capabilities and profits of the farmers and sharecroppers which would have devastated families and result in poverty. Wow!. That's not good I thought. I was six years old. Then I got older, I could read and my teacher was a little more objective about the situation. I learned that this in theory or at the rudimentary level was true. The North threatened the Souths' economic way of life and ultimately their culture. I also learned that in order for the South to continue their way of life they needed to keep and even grow the institution of slavery. Now I was still young, but, I had started taking Bible classes and knew that this was Biblically wrong. I also knew what happened to all the nations throughout history who enslaved people. Okay the Confederacy wanted to keep their plantation mansions and pretty dresses. But at the expense of people lives. Round one to the North. Did they want to end slavery because they were all righteous? Not all of them, but that conversation is for a different time. So, did the South petition the government and have peaceful demonstrations? Did they have a Savannah Cotton Party? No, they tried to denounce their government and attempted a hostile secession from the already established nation. The nation their forefathers painstakingly started. After a half a million deaths, the North was victorious, slavery ended. Happy ending? Of course not. Humanity and equality was still ignored. Well that is all about the Civil War. It had nothing to do with the principles of Jesus or any lesson of New Testament. The insurrection actually ignored the lessons of man being delivered from bondage in the Old Testament as well. Just as the insurrection on January 6th 2021.

I will include something else with the era of the Civil War. The Ku Klux Klan. After the American Civil War of 1861–1865, former Confederate soldiers and a few sympathetic to the Confederate cause, organized the KKK. Yes, they all considered themselves good Christian folk. The organization supposedly started as a social club, which was taken over in the next year by the hooded night people. It then began engaging in arson, beatings, destruction of property, lynching, murder, rape, tar-and-feathering, whipping, and voter intimidation. They targeted newly freed slaves, the occupying Union army and yes' even those nerdy Christians. That iteration of the Klan disappeared by the 1870s, but in 1915 a new Protestant-led iteration of the

Klan was formed in Georgia, during a period of xenophobia and anti-Catholicism. This version of the Klan vastly expanded both its geographical reach and its list of targets over those of the original Klan. Oh, and just to repeat myself, most members of the KKK identified or professed to be Christians. From an early time onward, the goals of the KKK included an intent to "reestablish Protestant Christian values in America by any means possible", and it believed that "Jesus was the first Klansman". Utterly ignorant, stupid and censored! Although members of the KKK swear to uphold Christian morality, virtually every Christian denomination has officially denounced the KKK. The ritual of lighting crosses was steeped in Christian symbolism, including prayer and hymn singing. I will stop writing about the KKK for they have an important role to play in the next chapter. Let me state this again. Our nation was never founded to be, a totally Christian nation based on historic or even Biblical text. Now if you noticed I used the word "totally". Our founding fathers explicitly and clearly excluded any reference to "God" or "the Almighty" or any euphemism for a higher power in the Constitution. Not one time is the word "god" mentioned in our founding document. Not one time. Many of the founding fathers denied the existence of Christ, owned slaves and signed measures to rid the land of Native Americans. By this I mean as a nation the majority of the population identifies as Christian. Our government, economy, and social structure as well as our global philosophy is based on the very rational and intellectual principles designed to foster our globally famous or infamous capitalistic system. So as we move further toward debating was America founded on the basis of Christianity let us begin by considering what, exactly, would have constituted a Christian Founding? My contention is merely that Christianity may have had an insignificant influence on America's Founders but this slight influence turned out to be a very significant event.

What are things besides a false understanding of our nation's founding that people usually point out when saying America is a Christian nation? One thing is money. Our nation being the richest of all and the fact that "In God We Trust" is on money. Even though that seems mutually exclusive of Biblical teaching. "In God We Trust" was first placed on United States coins, during the Civil War. This happened as a concession to show to the citizens of America and the world that despite the insurrection, there were true Christians in our country. It was not until a was law passed by the 84th Congress 1956 and "In God We Trust" was adopted as the national motto. What about the Pledge of Allegiance? The clause "under God" in the Pledge of Allegiance was inserted only in 1954, when President Eisenhower signed legislation to recognize "the dedication of our Nation and our people to the Almighty." But conservatives, ignorant of our history, or willfully ignoring it, wish us to believe that the pledge always referenced God. Many politicians wrongly attribute that clause with our founding fathers, stating, "If the pledge was good enough for the founding fathers, its good enough for me and I'll fight in defense of our Pledge of Allegiance." I guess they think the founders were alive in 1954. Also the verse "One nation under God, with liberty and justice for all" I am really, really confused about the hypocrisy of it all.

There are also the main songs passed down through generations which represent the pride and honor we have as a country. The Star Spangled Banner was written during the War of 1812. It was adopted as the national anthem by a congressional resolution on March 3, 1931. There was another song "Battle Hymn of the Republic", also known as "Mine Eyes Have Seen the Glory". This song was written to actually speak of how God was unhappy about the injustices in America, though it has been used as a hymn against prejudicial ideologies.

Faith led many Founders to conclude that religious liberty should be extensively protected. By the late 18th century, some Founders were beginning to question the wisdom of religious establishments, primarily because they thought that such establishments hurt true religion.

So did America have a Christian Founding? History is complicated, and we should always be suspicious of simple answers to difficult questions.

I may have spent way too much time writing about the founding fathers and early America to set the stage for what was to come. Namely divisions of political views, societal and economic classes and religious divisions which have led many Americans down an unrecoverable dark path.

The Bible as well as other religious text taught us that God would shine a light and protect those who believed. Jesus taught all those who followed the principles of love and humanity would be blessed, even though they may suffer in a cruel world. It does not follow that Americans would simply forget about their country's Christian roots. Anyone interested, in an accurate account of the nation's past cannot afford to ignore the important influence of faith, as well as false faith on many Americans, from the Puritans to the present day. It is a shame that not all human beings were included in Washington's letter, thoughts and prayer. If we think or surmise that America was meant to be an equal, just democratic nation, it has drifted from many intended principles. We would do well to reconsider the wisdom of these changes. The founding fathers worked hard to find the right mix, the right degree of their support for religion and how it would support the public. They also worked hard to ensure that religion freedom could coexist with all citizens, the local governments and the soon to blossom economy. This seems to be a conundrum even today.

Now I spent a lot of time focusing on how Christianity spread, and the founding of America. The Bible existed prior to and during the forming of America's first government. I spent a lot of time discussing the founding fathers and their take on the place of religion in government. Despite their personal belief and their hypocritical take on human rights, they formed a nation that would both flourish and continue for centuries to come. And ironically, at the same time, divide early America. You see the Bible shows us that nations and rulers were destroyed who ignored God teachings. Also destroyed, were those nations led by false preachers and fake Christians. Nations are not destroyed because of the clothes one wears or the music they listen to. We know that throughout history those who sought to adopt true Christian values were ridiculed and even murdered. Those who wavered and drunk the kool-aid flourished and prospered. Is that a good thing? Though economic prosperity can be a good thing, the politics and the need for economic entrepreneurship shaped and distorted what Jesus wanted of his children. This is evident from the Old to New Testament, early Christianity and as we will see even in today's political world. It is the transformation of religion, throughout thousands of years, that has birthed what today is the definition of the word systemic. Thousands of years of twisting and falsely preaching God's word became the DNA of America. I feel it is with the concern for the truth and understanding that I state, that though I am going to focus on the far right thinking legislators almost all whom have adopted certain political and economic world views have contributed to our nation's questionable righteousness.

Now in the early years of our political maturation, the Northern states were primarily Republican and the lower Southern states were Democratic. In the big picture it all evens out and not that important. They were all mainly professed Christians. The current acts of the far right derived from the old Democratic party. So you see when I move to discuss current America I am not trying to disparage a particular political group. I am however going to give objective fact, based on the teachings of Jesus and our current political system. What should be noted, is that Christian values and America's economic growth would dramatically change the political parties and our views of what Christianity means. We saw that throughout history the meaning and the purpose of the Gospels was driven by monarchial self-interest. After all the religious history and all the teachings and laws in the New World, I ask. Where did it lead ?

Christianity in the United States was developed or I should say, institutionalized, in concert with the combination of policies, and the political thinking of the country's forefathers. From the landing of the first European on Native American soil, to the country's independence, to the framing of the country's government and the unequal socio-economic constitution, America was destined to be what she is today. If we look at the Bible and then the changes to the principles of the teachings, we can see a slow turn toward a blueprint of national self-interest and hypocrisy. Throughout history good and godly men had to beg and even die for justice. There were also those who forged ahead and laid the groundwork for the establishment of the economy. Their importance whether Christian or not would have a long lasting effect on the economic system we covet today.

I feel we need to discuss the outlined ramifications of how our nation was founded. We all know there were no laws at the time which precluded the massacre and displacement of an entire race of people, namely Native Americans. There were also no constitutional laws forbidding slavery and or the unjust treatment of Chinese. This alone though played an instrumental role in the growth, development and wealth of a great portion of American society, it was not the only ground work laid by our fore-fathers which enabled the future sustainment of out capitalistic economy.

Going back prior to the colonization of the native land there were trading companies, Dutch, India, Russia and Turkey. The Dutch and East Indian merchants were able to get oil, spices and silk from Asia, where Russia and Turkey could not. The Dutch flourished and Europe afforded them the right to settle colonies as well as the right to supply goods throughout the entire "new" world. The most well known to some, is the Hudson Bay Company whom also controlled the fur trade in the colonies. When you watch movies about settlers or westerner going to the dry goods stores, those stores were stocked by one of these trading companies. Most likely Hudson Bay. The company was later acquired by Canada where it still exist. Many more companies used this business model and many more companies throughout the eighteenth and nineteenth centuries flourished. Other companies that flourished and branched off to be mega-farming institutes were plantations. As the colonies formed a nation there were inventions and businesses of practicality. Railroads, telegraphs, banks and newspapers. After the Civil War and in the dawn of the twentieth century there was an unprecedented industrial boom. Automobiles, airplanes, appliances and food sources would bring us into our current booming and unequal economy. There was an excellent historically based TV show, "The Men Who Built America", which touched on how the super upper class or 1% came into existence. Namely John D. Rockefeller, Cornelius Vanderbilt, Andrew Carnegie, Henry Ford and J.P. Morgan. They were great men whom had a vision and fulfilled their goals. They used the resources that were afforded to them to excel and literally become part of America's foundation. Would I say they were not Christian? Of course not. I do not know anything about them to dispute that. I will ask everyone can you be immoral and still be a Christian. My point is that many used the unequal laws and opportunities to accomplish their dreams. These unequal laws and opportunities were grown from the tree of America's unjust social and economic foundation. The seeds of this tree were revolution, separation of state and church, slavery, indentured servitude, confederacy and the proliferation of low income, middle income and upper income neighborhoods and societal classifications. Again, face value, non-Christian? No, I would not claim that. I would question it. But, what these policies and ways of thinking enabled could justifiably be classified as non-Christian. It speaks to the term inherent, ingrained and systematic. After four hundred years, you could say that immigrants being separated from the babies, social injustice or African Americans being shot in the back are our fault. Why? Wait a minute. I say it is our fault because we continue to do things in the law abiding peaceful way. The Christian way. The peaceful way antithesis of the way our country operates. Now before you raise your eyebrows, I am not calling for a military coupe. I am reminding everyone of the injustices and persecution the righteous will endure. The only way a people will be treated as Jesus intended is if they lived amongst those who respect humanity. But as policies continue to be enacted we can clearly see our country is moving away from Christian values faster than any time in my lifetime. We are forgetting our obligations to care for the elderly, the fatherless, the widows and the sick. We forgot our obligation to take care of the land we were blesses with. And we forgot our obligation to love those not like us. Let's take a look.

We started with the Old Testament where God, punished those who did not show Him the love He deserved. God also punished entire nations, entire populations. Then we moved to the New Testament where Jesus showed love and compassion to those who were mistreated and downtrodden. Hopefully, we took note that just about all God's chosen leaders were men and women from sorted questionable past. None stood in front of listeners shouting of their righteousness or great anointing. After Jesus, we saw Christianity take a turn and begin to resemble what God and Jesus feared. False prophets, rich churches and abuse of the average citizen. Then as the Church of England and the Roman Catholic Church grew in power and influence people fled to the Land of Milk and Honey. Not the Biblical land but America and things became topsy turvy. America started its history with atheist, deist, Christians and radical Christians. Yes radical Christians.

We are now ready to dive into present day politics and religion. A present day born out of centuries of manipulation of laws, people and God's word.

Chapter Five

Christianity in Todays Society

ow we have an overview of both the how the Bible teaches us about how we should act and respect others as well as how the teachings of Jesus became political, worldly or maybe just subjective. We discussed how this blossomed into spiritual teaching and became what we have termed today as religion. We also discussed how religion played a role in the framing of our Constitution and the foundation of our nation. If we put all these things together we will either understand and or be confused about the current views, policies and lifestyles our great nation has adopted. Has our country corrected its wrong path and treat each other in the manner we define our nation? Do we as a Christian nation, align with the original teachings of Jesus or have we slowly followed the path history has led us down? The fork in the road. The no light at the end of the tunnel. The straight path to Revelation. And no, I am not holding a sign claiming the end is near! Inevitable maybe.

As I point out contradictions in political behavior with Christian values, I am going to point out what many Far Right Republicans, few Democrats and citizens believe. I will also discuss the policies they support and the consequences these policies have had on the health of our nation. Why? Because their thinking along with years of influence is what has shaped our country and is the catalyst behind our countries views, opinions and appearance. And let me firmly state that some Democrats, Independents and even atheists are as well, complicit in my confusion. But I've never quite understood where a lot, not all, of the true far right Republicans get off claiming Christianity. While condoning the things that they do. Fact. I have spoken to many Conservative Christians of varied races, all of whom condone Trump's approval of neo-nazis, communist dictators, call for violent protest and attack peaceful protesters. Do they speak of being Christian because they go to church? Because many of them can quote scripture? The devil can quote scripture! Because they say they are in front of a podium? Or, is it they just support the Constitution? I point out that the Constitution is not a Christian document. And, for anyone citing a few words mentioning religion, then I ask, "Have we supported the ideas of freedom and equality in the documents which are the foundation of our nation?" Many policies they support and the bills they try to pass sure as heck do not represent real Christian values. To know what should be supported, one must have the intelligence to know what Christian values are. More on that later, as well. I guess their opposition to abortion and gay rights is where they stake their biggest claim to following "Christianity." Or maybe the 2nd Amendment is their claim to being a true Christian? Why not? Being able to carry tactical weapons is a really what Jesus died for. Legally being able to justify killing unarmed citizens may be Constitutional, but not Christian. Have we supported equality for all? That is a rhetorical question. Of course we haven't. Instead, we have supported political views, opinions, emotional decisions and historic racist values. Let me make sure everyone understands. I am not saying everyone in America is racist or supports racist policies. I am saying the country has been historically viewed, and known as holding on to racist philosophies. That is why I constantly refer to the nation. Not individuals. To further qualify, I will add, I am confused if they know, accept or separate their political duties from their Christian obligations. To that fact, I even question some evangelical preachers, regardless of political affiliation. Being a Christian does not simply mean going to church and following five scriptures in the Bible. It is not having a television broadcast and collecting millions of dollars. No matter how many people tune in and give their hard earned money. As always, I will qualify. Make the millions but be ready to do what Jesus ask. Give it all away to the needy. It definitely is not adhering to policies or amendments that are obviously anti-Christian. It is not supporting lies and blasphemous accusations. Christianity is defined by, believing in, and following the Word, of Jesus Christ. And guess what? Jesus did not talk justifying murder. Whether by gun rights or the death penalty. He did talk about love for all, including gay-rights, including third world countries. Excuse me using the term "third world". He said the love of the Lord is for everyone. He also said blessed are the poor in spirit, the meek, those who are persecuted and those who thirst for righteousness. What does righteousness mean? For you to judge your conviction to Christianity based on abortion or gun rights or even capitalism means you're assuming that Jesus would support the capitalistic ideology of associating wealth with greatness, greatness with wealth and wealth at the sake of the poor. Maybe you think you are smarter than Jesus was.

There is also a term used by many Christians based on false understanding of the Bible. I would like to point out that many use the term values incorrectly. There are economic values as well as ethic and social values. A value in terms of economics is something that provides a physical but yet, relative benefit to the individual consumer. There are also subjective social values. Values derived from the subjective opinions, taste and desired norms set by the majority. Whether moral or immoral. In Christianity a value is relates to more ethical and spiritual things. It could be something that positively affects person's well-being, physically, emotionally and spiritually. When some Christians speak of values they mistakenly refer to things like the clothes, people wear. The style of their hair. They do not refer to inhumanity or the economic cause of someone's choices. I personally witnessed an example of how a church praised their sense of values. Ironically, enough prior to the fire The pastor at a church denigrated youth for their dress and slang terms. Through a chorus of amen, he slammed the values of the youth as well as their parents. He also lifted up his lacky parishioners who wore suits and gave huge tithes. After the service the church caught fire and many youth and babies were in the basement. Who do you think ran back in the church to save the children? The youth who were just humiliated by the church. Who do you think stood outside and watched? The high and mighty men of great values. Who actually had showed the greatest values? Who do you think would be the ones Jesus took to walk beside Him? Maybe you know what Jesus feels about values. Maybe you are more woke, than Jesus was. Isn't it quite arrogant for anyone to assume they would know what the son of God would believe on issues of today, that are not repeated through His words? Worse, it is quite scary someone would twist the words of God. Good news though, Jesus did openly speak about many of the values which he did, in fact, support. However, many of those aren't reflected in the way many conservatives act and they're surely not found in many of the policies supported by the GOP.

To showcase the hypocrisy between the words of Jesus and the current state of our beloved country, I thought I'd run through some key traits which I've come to understand that Jesus Christ strongly supported. I will raise the question whether or not the immoral majority represents teaching we have discussed. If we claim to be followers of Christ, we should abide by God's Word. If we are a Christian nation then our country's decisions should be based on God's Word, not the Second Amendment. As children of God, we should follow our Constitution and laws, but we should not forsake God's word to do such. And where many circumvent laws, because they can or because of loopholes they should consider their spiritual fate. Our decisions should be faith based and not politically based. The political party one choses should be a closely aligned with God's word. And, not a few made up scriptures, falsely misquoting and realigning the scripture. One must look at the entire scripture, verse, chapter, and book. There are plethora of scriptures that warn against this. Luckily, the Bible can be summarized in two commandments. Love God and love others. Every way we should act, everything we should do, stems from those simple edicts. To keep myself from going on a tangent I will try to point out just a few things focusing on three topics. First are spiritual attributes we should have learned from the Bible and should have learned from all the preachers and pastors. This is where we dive into the Gifts and Fruits of the Spirit. If you remember in Isaiah and Galatians respectively. First a quick breakdown distinguishing and given a comparison of the two. The Gifts of the Spirit were first revealed in the Old Testament. They were given to man to in order to build him or her up so they may be wise and faithful servants to God. These Gifts which were supposed to be available immediately, were given to believers that they would have the capabilities to begin, grow and flourish in the ministry to others.

"The Spirit of the LORD will rest on Him, The spirit of wisdom and understanding, The spirit of counsel and strength, The spirit of knowledge, piety, and the fear of the LORD." Isaiah 11:2

Not to confuse anyone or get to wordy the Bible also speaks about how these gifts are manifested. One's anointing should be evident by the manifestations of his or her be filled with knowledge, speak and act with wisdom, Gift of Prophecy, Gift of Faith, Gifts of Healing. Being able to perform miracles, discerning of Spirits, speaking in tongues and interpreting tongues. This can be found in first Corinthians. Let me elaborate on the manifestations and give my own degree of wisdom. The Bible teaches us that these manifestations are given freely and independently to each individual already blessed with the Gifts. Why is this important? One reason is the gift is from God or the Holy Spirit. Not man or the palms of a man's hands. In today's society many try to manipulate people and prey on his or her weaknesses and mental state. All I will say is it is easy for a pastor to get ten thousand followers to believe they are speaking in tongues. It is a lot harder to convince believers that they actually prophesized or performed miracle, though those things, according to the Bible, are equally available and given to us by the Holy Spirit. Ok, let me move on.

There is also the Fruits of the Spirit. Unlike the Gifts, which are freely given, the Fruits develop over time. They are manifested by one's change of his or her character. Once we become Christian, not profess to be, the Holy Spirit will slowly change our character. One of the most important things to change will be how we view and treat others. The most recognized fruits of the Spirit are love, joy, peace, patience, kindness, goodness, faithfulness, gentleness, and self-control.

We will first focus on certain Fruits of the Spirit. Instead of going through each separately I am going to discuss actions things like appreciating everyone and everything, giving and not taking, caring for the land we profess God blessed us with, being honest and truthful, being kind and loving all created by God, and taking care of the poor, elderly and sick. These are things that The second thing we will discuss are policies our leaders fight for, enact and subvert. Policies enacted that either represent or are mutually exclusive to the principles of the Fruits of the Spirit. Third will be behaviors we have shown within our own country and to the rest of the world. Behaviors that may not be publicized or even admitted. Behaviors that plague us when viewed by other countries.

The first thing I am going to tackle is the love and respect we need to have for God and subsequently for all others. This attribute encompasses all we will later discuss. Things like our appreciation, our caring and our love for each other. Do you know how many verses there are in the Bible about loving God? Over one hundred. Do you have any idea how many verses there are about loving one another? Read the Bible. Many people who say they love God and the Bible do not have the intelligence to realize how many of those verses actually give instructions on how we should show this love and appreciation. To all humanity.

"Beloved, let us love one another, for love is from God, and whoever loves has been born of God and knows God. Anyone who does not love, does not know God, because God is love. Beloved, if God so loved us, we also ought to love one another" 1 John 4:7-21 ESV. I am not sure what to write about this, because it seems so simple, obvious and downright elementary. There are many other things we can talk about, that are emblematic or characteristic of showing ones love to God and others. What is the extent of loving God? It is being appreciative, try your best to live in accordance to His will and show love to others. Better stated, show the same love to all, no matter what economic status, race, creed, religion or sex. Show the same love to them as you would show God.

How does the Bible teach us we should show our love for God? How does the Bible teach us we should show our love for our fellow man? How do people show their love for God and their fellow man? Many people attempt to show their appreciation and love God just by going to church or by tithing. But, would not support a youth selling lemonade to help his family. I searched the Bible about church and more specifically about going to church. Yes, there are scripture about meeting and gathering with like men of faith. There are no scriptures by way of any command or law. If they only way you can be around true, honest, like individuals is by going to church, then you need to change your environment and friends. The Old Testament has the most scriptures about tithing. Pastors use many of them today. Many of them use those Old Testament scripture incorrectly. As in the condemnation of robbing God. The Old Testament speaks how tithes were to be used to fill the storehouse, so God's people would not go hungry. Christian's use tithing as evidence of their generosity and is often done because they are told they need to tithe to stay in the good graces of God. Some do so because the truly believe it will be used for God's work. Some do so to be given favor amongst their congregation or parishioners. And unfortunately some do so to impress themselves. Giving should be done to bless others less fortunate and in need. Do you know that a tithe can be giving ten percent of your salary to help God's people? The few scriptures on tithing have been somewhat twisted.. It is an individual thing. Just to make sure everyone understands that tithing is neither a gift, fruit nor a command. I give the utmost respect to those who do so hoping the money will feed the hungry as oppose to buy someone a new car or plane. Because you tithe doesn't mean you're being generous or giving. Especially when you're giving out of obligation to your religion, not an unwavering generosity and willingness to help those who you may disagree with their beliefs or lifestyle. But simply help them because they are in need. And not a tax deduction. In Luke a Pharisee boast about tithing and Jesus basically tells him, so what! Can you tithe and still rob God? What do you think? So all that said, how do we show we love God? By loving one another before all things.

One thing that repeatedly got the Israelites in hot water with God was they did not show their appreciation for His grace, mercy and blessings. They claimed they loved God, but their actions show differently. They made sacrifices, said their prayers and did not eat pork. But we should understand none of those things show love. Again, the New Testament makes it clear that doing things on the surface but not truly being appreciative, thankful and obedient is a recipe for disaster. Following the crowd even if it is the majority will end in disaster. Christians are called to remember that everything they have is a gracious gift from God. That is things we received from Him and not things we strong–armed, stole, swindled or took from various ethnicities because our laws condoned those acts. Just like the Israelites, we should not think that blessing we received mean we have a license to act stupid. The Biblical doctrine is called common grace, a concept that everything good in life is an unearned gift from God. By unearned I mean you did not actually deserve the gift, but it was given to you nonetheless. Everything good in life is not necessarily a G5 private jet. Even though if I could afford one I probably would buy one. How one defines earnings versus gifts is a matter of perspective. For those who argue that he or she worked so hard, and achieved everything on his or her own, should really think about that. What successes are earned without the help of family, friends, mentors, geography, socioeconomic status, ethnicity, genetic composition or culture? I would venture very few, if any. The Christian, therefore, has no moral high-ground by which to judge himself above others. I do therefore implore everyone to remember the Israelites. Additionally, the Bible teaches us that worth and equality for all mankind is based on the principle that God created us in his image. I have been unfortunate to witness many judging others as if they were the only ones created in God's image. This means that someone born into poverty is worth the same as someone born into extreme wealth. Someone who suffered through the foster system is worth the same as someone born to stable family. One's background or demographic characterization does not change or determine the value or worth of that individual. If all lives have equal value, then there should be equality among all Christians in the area of human rights., political representation, healthcare and economic capabilities And to be real this should apply to all humans, not just Christians. And the fact that it does not and people are still oppressed basically guarantees the fulfillment of the last book of the Bible.

Another aspect of love is our obligation to be tolerant, respectful and acceptant. "Put on then, as God's chosen ones, holy and beloved, compassionate hearts, kindness, humility, meekness, and patience" Col. 3:12 ESV. Throughout time, man has been against anyone with a different religion, ethnicity gender or even social class. There is no distinction in the Bible and we are not given a pass just because we agree or disagree with someone. Nations and political leaders should also care how the world views them, but many do not. That is even scarier. Let me ask those who dislike Trump. Is it because of his ethnicity, race or because he repeatedly proves he does not value or respect the inherent rights of all races, ethnicities, genders and beliefs? What do you think Jesus's view would be of someone who disrespects and degrades others? Those who blindly believes everything he says and does, why? When I speak of treating everyone with respect I will again remind readers I am talking about globally. All races and ethnicities. A president representing a Christian nation should not dishonor our professed beliefs by making disparaging, disrespectful, un-God-like comments he makes about other races, countries, beliefs and persons. Trump had an extensive list of comments about African American, Mexicans, Hispanics, Native Americans, Muslims, Jews, immigrants, women, and people with disabilities. "They're bringing drugs. They're bringing crime. They're rapists. And some, I assume, are good people". He tweeted fake statistics claiming that African Americans are responsible for the majority of murders of whites, and in some speeches he linked African Americans and Hispanics with violent crime. Unfortunately, we cannot spend the pages to go through them all in detail. But many Christians do not even think those comments are wrong. Many conservative Christians support this behavior. Why am I talking about Trump now? Because the country has done things and supported actions that clearly indicate that Trump may once again be president.

Let's look at the message of treating all the children of God with equal love, equal treatment. When I reference all of God's children, I am referring to all men and women. Love for all means respecting all. Love for all means equal rights for all, equal treatment, equal access and equal opportunity. But, we know where our country stands on that view, compared to other Christianity countries. This could be a separate book. What should we discuss? The rights of African Americans from slavery to Jim Crow to prison? The rights of Blacks not to be murdered by police? The rights of Central and South Americans to leave a violent condition? Maybe we could discuss the rights of Americans to carry tactical weapons? Really! What about the rights of the LBGT community to live an existence free from ridicule? Or the rights of white nationalist to shout racial epitaphs. Do not think so! We could discuss the lack of equal rights for women to include opportunity and salary. Why as a country should women had to fight for equal rights and actually continue to fight? How about other predominantly Christian nations? How does America stack up to other Christian nations as far as equal rights? Not well.

When did equal rights laws come into effect? We know that many individual rights were parsed out over years. Was Christian America, established on the premise of equal rights for all? Or was it established based on the premise of equal rights for some? This is more of a rhetorical question, since we already discussed. Was it established based on love for all or love for some? What did it take to enact laws or bills that gave legal equal rights to many? For most racial, gender and groups it took many centuries. How many lives were lost fighting for these rights? Hundreds of thousands. Were equal rights given, because of our love of Christ or because of revolution, war, civil disobedience and mass protest? Many rights were obtained after protest and the imprisonment and death of those seeking justice. Most laws regarding equal rights were achieved through sweat, pain, sacrifice and even lives. It seems like today equal rights or humane rights will only be considered if there is an economic impact or the right's bottom line is affected. How many years of inequality did and are we experiencing? Is inequality historical or Christian? Does inequality arise because of a form of religion, an economic system or a form of Christianity? Yes I separated religion and Christianity. There are many questions to ask. But only one conclusion. The inequality inflicted, caused by false preachers, teachers, kings, forefathers and nations is based on the weaponization of true Christianity. This caused the dilution of many of the characterizations and adaptation of Christian values. When I use the term fore-fathers I am not just talking about the "founding" fathers. When I use the term weaponization I am simply referring to using it as a means to gain a powerful advantage and to subdue or pacify someone or a group of people. I think it is again time to state I am not talking about all Christians or all persons of faith. When I question Christianity I am speaking about today and not the New Testament truth of what Christianity should have been and should be.

Keeping consistent with the biblical theme when was inequality first mentioned or introduced in the Bible? We all should be certain that it came to our attention in the Old Testament. From the Land of Canaan and beyond. If you have read the Bible or even this book, you should know that the Old and New Testament showed us that nations never supported equality. Only Jesus actually practiced treating individuals equally, irrespective of their background. This inequality seemed to be a major part of the socio-political machine throughout all time. And for sure throughout Americas past and even present. "Here there is not Greek and Jew, circumcised and uncircumcised, barbarian, Scythian, slave, free; but Christ is call, and in all" Col 3:11 ESV

Though our country forcibly ended the inequality of slavery there is still inequality. Though our country reversed its laws regarding woman's right to vote, there is still inequality. Though certain gay rights were given there is still inequality. It is important to remember most freedoms took wars, protest, courts and death before being granted. None were granted because of the love of one's brother. In our freedom of religion country there is still inequality for many Jews, Muslims, Atheist and others. And though our country claims to be Christian and show love for all, there is still inequality and social barriers that accept unequal treatment of Blacks by certain police officers. What many fail to understand sometimes no matter how one relatively or qualitatively defines inequality it boils down to a lack of sensitivity. I guess it will take something more than Jesus words to overturn or support the equality for all races, genders, life-styles, economically disadvantaged, countries and political systems. Ok. So now Trump is no longer President and a new administration is in power. Can conclude our country is ready to resume and forge ahead with its equal treatment and universal brotherly love? But hold your horses. Our country is still what it is. Is Jesus clapping His hands? Is He applauding our country's reversal of depravity and history of inequality?

Before I forget, let's discuss how the poor are generally treated. I say generally because there are wonderful organizations and individuals that assist and care for the poor. As a country, not as much. I guess that is why so many individuals start non-profits and foundations to care or others. God's special interest in the poor is expressed throughout the New Testament. God's Son came as a poor man, lived as a poor man, and died as a poor man. That is by our standards. Though abundantly rich with favor, faith and peace. He was good news to the poor. Jesus cared deeply about the impoverished. Caring for the poor is the second thing I should mention. Also, remember who Jesus walked with and trusted. If you do not know, please read the bible. We will later talk about the effects of poverty and how those statistics affect world views.

Most Christians think the poor are sinful hell bound people. Many Christians point to passages in the New Testament, from the verse in Thessalonians that says, "The one who is unwilling to work shall not eat". I guess they are the ones who learn scripture for his or her benefit. Which is repeatedly admonished throughout the scriptures. Jesus' appeal to care for needy are echoed in Matthew, Mark and John, "The poor you will always have with you." What does that mean? In my eyes... "Get over it... the poor will always exist in this world we have adopted" In this world, is why He came in the first place. To be sure, the persistence of poverty is not a reason to ignore the plight of the poor, but to draw near to them with generosity. Deuteronomy 15:11 tells us, "There will always be poor people in the land. Therefore I command you to be openhanded toward your fellow Israelites who are poor and needy in your land." Christians' wide varying viewpoint stems from a theological divide with scripture and the economy in the early 20th century. Biblically we are told that one's response to poverty should be generosity and openhandedness. Am I saying everyone should forfeit their wealth or extra dollars to make sure no one is poor? No. Not at all. I am saying those who shout and self glorify our nation as the greatest Christian nation in the world, we could do better. Better, buy just caring more. Do not fight to pay someone a wage where they can not feed their family because one wants to selfishly make as much money as they can.

The more I read and understand scripture I realize that we own the problems of the impoverished as much as they do. We must realize that our inactions and overall social inequalities may have created many of problems of the poor. We are all at fault for the state of our world. But we can also join Jesus in changing the state of our world.

Does our country address the condition of poverty and meet the needs of the poor according to the scripture? Let us look at a few bible verses.

Deuteronomy 15:10 (NIV) "Give generously to them and do so without a grudging heart; then because of this the LORD your God will bless you in all your work and in everything you put your hand to."

Proverbs 19:17 (NIV) "Whoever is kind to the poor lends to the LORD, and he will reward them for what they have done."

Proverbs 22:9 (NIV) - "The generous will themselves be blessed, for they share their food with the poor."

Isaiah 58:10 (NIV) - "And if you spend yourselves in behalf of the hungry and satisfy the needs of the oppressed, then your light will rise in the darkness, and your night will become like the noonday."

2 Corinthians 9:6-7 (NIV) - "Remember this: Whoever sows sparingly will also reap sparingly, and whoever sows generously will also reap generously. Each of you should give what you have decided in your heart to give, not reluctantly or under compulsion, for God loves a cheerful giver."

Proverbs 14:31 (NIV "He who oppresses the poor shows contempt for their Maker, but whoever is kind to the needy honors God."

Luke, as is well known, had a particular concern for the poor as the subjects of Jesus' compassion and ministry. In his version of the Beatitudes, the poor are blessed as the inheritors of God's kingdom even as the corresponding curses are pronounced to the rich.

On the other side of the coin of this topic is the wealthy. Not so much as those with wealth but the love of wealth that cause many to ignore, belittle and exploit those without. Jesus explicitly condemns excessive love of wealth as an intrinsic evil in various passages in the Gospels, especially in Luke. He also consistently warns of the danger of riches as a hindrance to favor with God; as in the Parable of the Sower, where it is said:

"And the cares of this world, and the deceitfulness of riches, and the lusts of other things entering in; it chokes the Word, which becomes unfruitful" Mark 4:19 (KJV)

In the story of Jesus and the rich young man the young ruler's wealth inhibits him from following Jesus and thereby attaining the Kingdom. When questioned, Jesus comments on the young man's discouragement was simple. "How hard it is for the rich to enter the kingdom of God! Indeed, it is easier for a camel to go through the eye of a needle than for someone who is rich to enter the kingdom of God." Those who heard this were astonished, "Who then can be saved?", they asked. Jesus replied, "Stick with God." What does that mean? If God is Love then I guess you stick with Love.

In the Sermon on the Mount and the Sermon on the Plain, Jesus the crowd to sell their earthly goods and give to the poor. And they will provide themselves with "a treasure in heaven that will never fail, where no thief comes near and no moth destroys" and he adds "For where your treasure is, there will your heart be also" (Lk 12.34 NIV)

And Jesus adds, "This is how it will be with whoever stores up things for themselves but is not rich toward God" (Lk 12.21 NIV)

Jesus and Zacchaeus is an example of storing up heavenly treasure, and being rich toward God. The repentant tax collector Zacchaeus not only welcomes Jesus into his house but joyfully promises to give half of his possessions to the poor, and to rebate overpayments four times over if he defrauded anyone.

Why do we not live as we say we believe and live as Jesus taught? What we do with our beliefs is as important to Jesus as what we believe. Jesus is about complete commitment to loving him and others. Jesus loves belief- filled actions, as his saying to not only a wealthy young man but, shows, but to all wealthy people who questioned His message and His purpose. Jesus is not suggesting it is impossible for a rich person to enter the kingdom of heaven, or be saved. He is saying it is only possible with God. And for God to enter a person's life they must be open to Him entering. And that, is one of the points of my inquisition. How must one act for God to enter his or her life. What principles of morality and simple humanity must a person possess? And if our mission in life is wealth then our judgement will be based on that. Many of us are just like the rich young man. Out of one side of our mouth we speak allegiance to Jesus, but out of the other side we're speaking allegiance to the trappings of wealth. I know, because the rich young man asks the same questions I would ask. Jesus specifically tells a man that all his wealth, respected for others and observing the Ten Commandments is lacking. Jesus tells the man that he lacks self-sacrifice for others. He lacks giving to the extent that it is painful to him. He lacks an ability to put aside his wealth for the sake of the gospel. If Jesus believed that belief is about action, why do not we? Why have we not dedicated ourselves to bringing true discipleship and love to others, when it is what Christ told us to do? What good is belief without it offering true hope? Hope is what the country and the world needs. We have become complacent with the state of world affairs and convinced ourselves that those in power causing division and inhumanity are the true conservative Christian.

God has asked us to demonstrate our belief by bringing good news to those who feel hopeless. What good news does our country give others? I am talking about good news that is quantifiable. We are called to drop everything for Him and take the chance to do what is right and just. Jesus envisions what the world could look like and calls us to join God in the process of making that vision a reality. It is about exchanging the currencies of this world for the currency of love.

One must conclude that Jesus was an extra ordinary being, especially when it came to following the rules. Some say that the sins that cause a person to be in poverty may be the sins of others, not of the person who is poor. To elaborate, the sins of greediness, of economic structures and social disadvantages should be considered, a form of sin. As time progress the rapid growth of sinful nations led to the poverty of the common person. You have to live a life with other people in mind and you have to give freely. You cannot have one without the other. Oh, I guess if we applied that principle, we would be Socialist?

To further discuss love and acceptance we can look at another big swing and a miss for Far right Republicans. Besides lacking in showing love for all groups by acts of kindness another fault we see is their intent on judging and ridiculing others. Most of whom have different opinions, or so called values. Many people and even news personalities don't think this matters. In short, you just don't ridicule those God's children. From what I read this is a very important tenet of Christianity. Many politicians will judge and ridicule an opposing base just for votes. Votes for what? A political office or the free plane, chauffeur and hotel suite. At the expense of defaming Mexicans and other colored nationalities. They ridicule other races, ethnicities, genders and even their own Christian brethren. And if many believe in God's words as many say they do, then ridicule nations and profess love for Jesus they should know the consequences, based on the Bible. Last food for thought on the subject of treating people unequally. Was it the downtrodden, abused, enslaved, poor and meek whom God favored and redeemed throughout the Bible? Or, was it the rich God continually blessed and lifted up?

Well, Far right Republicans seem to be very judgmental and very disrespectful. Basically, if you're not a straight, white, church going male, who believes in two Constitutional Amendments you're judged. Let me clarify that certain whites are in the judged bucket as well. Also, quite a few minorities have drunk from the same trough and believe the divisive rhetoric. Some of the most vile, hateful, ignorant judgement I've ever witnessed came from those who held Congressional seats and professed to attending church frequently. It seems high church attendance gives these people the feeling that they're superior to others because they sit in a building and listen to someone tell them what is and isn't acceptable. I'm sure you know these types of people. The alcoholic, been divorced three times or beats his wife, angry, hateful, judgmental individual who goes around telling others what is morally right and wrong while making excuses for their own indiscretions in life. They have adulterous sex with minors, yell how nations should be bombed, and threaten other members of Congress. They sit in the front rows with their families and call themselves, "God fearing men". Yelling that the youth with his droopy pants who provides for his little siblings or visits and helps the elderly lady in his neighborhood is going to hell in a handbasket is falsely judgmental and dangerous. The youth with the droopy pants or the girl with the mini-skirt is no more sinful than the well-dressed crooked, abusive, cheating holier than thou person. Truth be told, I cannot stand the droopy pants! That is what being judgmental is. Passing judgement. Passing judgement prejudicially. Like you have the insight on everyone's heart and Jesus mercy. Ironically many of the politicians I am referring to not only justified the insurrection on January 6th, but actually assisted in ensuring its existence.

The MAGA Republican party transformed their social platform based on judging anyone who isn't just like they are and uplifting those whose moral compass is somewhat different. Do we as Christians believe in and defend the words of Jesus or the words of narcissists? Is our nation far removed or in agreement with the thoughts of our former President? He implied a moral equivalence between white supremacist marchers and those who protested against them. In 2018, during an Oval Office meeting about immigration reform, he referred to El Salvador, Haiti, and African countries as "shitholes". Trump sent a tweet suggesting to look into land seizures and the mass killing of white farmers in South Africa, acting on a racist conspiracy theory. That said, I will adamantly admit there are those who do respect all and those who attend church because they have a personal true relationship with God. And for them I thank you.

The problem with judging others is causes predetermined responses and actions. It causes some to treat others unfairly based on how they were judged whether justified or not. The worst thing is that if a group in power judges someone or another group, then you have millions committing a same fateful sin.

Another overlooked attribute is simply, being honest. In Exodus when the Ten Commandments was revealed to Moses, the eighth commandment was, "Thou shall not bear false witness against thy neighbor" I know, no one reading thinks this refers to a "witness" in a trial! King Solomon said, "False witness is among the six things God hates". He also said, "The lying witness is a deceitful man, who mocks at justice. He is like a war club, or a sword, or a sharp arrow. A false witness will not go unpunished. And he that tell lies shall persish". Proverbs 6:16–19 (NAS). Did former President Trump ever repent? What did he repented about? Or is he infallible? Or is he inhumane and never did anything that would require him to repent. If you believe that then you are not a true believer in the scriptures. There are six things that the LORD strongly dislikes, seven that are an abomination to him, they are haughty eyes, a lying tongue, and hands that shed innocent blood, a heart that devises wicked plans, feet that make haste to run to evil, a false witness who breathes out lies, and one who sows discord among brothers.

Do you need a little confirmation from the New Testament? Jesus said, "False testimony is among the things that defile a person". Lying as too the sincerity of someone is false testimony. Lying to defile ones name, place of birth or spiritual conviction is a lie. The Book of John the history of lying. "You are of your father the devil, and the desires of your father you want to do… he is a liar and the father of it" John 8:44 (NIV).

Lying without repentance and forgiveness leads to "the second death" described in Revelation, which says, "and all liars, their portion will be in the lake that burns with fire and sulfur, which is the second death." Revelation 21:8 (ESV).

Be faithful to the Bible's teachings and if you have lied, seek forgiveness from those to whom you have lied, and obey the Gospel, for "If we confess our sins, he is faithful and just to forgive us our sins, and to cleanse us from all unrighteousness" 1 John 1:9 (KJV)

Okay I guess everyone should get my point. I am shocked by how many people do not care if a President or anyone not only tells untruths, but makes false comments and accusations against individual. He even says these things about other Christians. Let me repeat one more time. Lying without repentance and forgiveness leads to "the second death" described in Revelation 21:8 (KJV), which says, "all liars shall have their part in the lake which burns with fire and brimstone, which is the second death". Be faithful to the Bible's teachings and if you have lied, seek forgiveness from those to whom you have lied, and obey the Gospel. How many times has the former President apologized or repented about his remarks or his lies? There have actually been too many lies and disparaging words out the mouth of our former President and other professed. Christians in our government to write about. Proverbs tell us "...a worthless and a wicked man...is a constant liar; he signals his true intentions to his friends with eyes and feet and fingers". I would like to request that readers do not try to argue about things they heard others say. That is unless they have facts, video or audio proof. Please no word of mouth, especially from a liar. What about either suing someone or threatening to sue someone. Is that the act of someone following Jesus teachings? First lies, then bearing false witness. I guess you are saying, Wow. He talked a lot about lying! Yes, lying shows a lack of remorse, compassion or even a conscience. Whether it is about the Mexico building of a wall, the effects of Covid and even more damaging was the lies about the election results, which led to the most mutually exclusive Christian act, an insurrection causing death. Let's not forget the lies about the insurrection being a tour, a hug fest, an act of a few protesters. And, of course, we will get into that a little more later. I do however feel bad for the millions of Christians who believed and acted on his lies instead of just embracing the Spirit freely given to them. You see lying is not limited to one sneaking a few doughnuts or lap dance. Last thing. When I bring this up to Trump supporters they retort, "well Obama lied too". They do not admit it is wrong. Instead they go the childish route and like an eight year old claim' "I know you are, but what am I"? Remember that?

Enough of that. The previous section the esoteric personality traits that should be evident in Christian's everyday living. But, now let us look at substantive policies, programs and institutions synonymous with the United States of America. We will also bring everything together and discuss what conditions exist in America that show our policies were designed to provide equality, love, safety, freedom and long life. Let us jump to policies that affect the lives of its citizens and the policies our elected officials put in place. First, does everyone know what I mean by policies put in place? I would like to keep things consistent and look at policies supported Fruits of the Spirit and the teachings of Jesus. We should know by now that certain administrations have supported policies that do the opposite. With the approval and support of their supporters and base.

What am I referring to when I use the term, policies? There are several definitions or types of policies. In general terms the Oxford definition is a course or principle of action adopted or proposed by a government, party, business, or individual. Also one should note that there are private and public policies. So a policy can be anything from the statement of a law, to a sign hung up in a window of a restaurant or country club refusing service to a specific race, creed or gender. A privately owned restaurant or sport teams can mandate that employees or persons using establishment must receive a COVID-19 vaccination. Where public institutions, with the exception of some government agencies, mandating mask wearing or vaccines will have a legal struggle to enforce.

Where do I begin on this policy topic? Remember we are now focusing on our nation as it is today. First, let me quickly remind everyone of the previous topic of our country's acts of discernment or attributes. The lack of nation-wide love and respect for all has influenced the policies our leaders promote and adopt. I will try to stay consistent with attributes previously mentioned to polices affecting our love for different races, the poor, the sick, our environment and the rest of the world. I will discuss equal rights first and then transition into poverty. The other short comings are somewhat a cause an effect of poverty. The need for the illusive fair wage and a fair chance to obtain a decent safe life, as well as the need to put profit before society ultimately leads to things like drugs, crime and lack of healthcare.

Now we will discuss Equal Rights policies. Since the inception of our country as an independent nation, there have been many, many bills and laws addressing equal rights. Before I dive into them, I will ask. If the foundation of the political framework is the Constitution and the moral framework is the Bible, why hasn't equal rights for all always existed? From the inception of our God fearing Christian nation, the Native Americans, Irish, Italians, Asians, African Americans, the poor and the down trodden have all been treated unequally. For many they still are till this day. Well I did forget conservative Christians do not believe in the inequality existing in the soil and soul of our nation.

There are volumes of policies we can discuss pertaining to equal rights or the lack thereof. Policies that allowed unequal treatment in housing, education, health, employment, safety and life in general. For most of these I will take a separate look at a few of these topics. In general the term equal rights wasn't even prevalent until the nineteen sixties. Hundreds of years after the forming of our Christian nation. Does everyone know that the

Equal Rights Amendment was not passed by the last state until the year 2020.

Instead of rehashing the acceptance of inequality in this country, I will discuss some of many executive orders that were needed just to address this problem in the year 2021. For all it is worth, President Biden signed an executive order to promote racial equity. I am not bringing this up to shout praise. Though due. I am bringing this up to bring attention to the fact that in the twenty first century, in a great Christian nation such an order is even necessary. I actually am confused about the "promote" part and not the absolute requirement.

Biden also ordered the government to conduct equity assessments of its agencies and reallocate resources for the purpose of ensuing people of color and others who have been historically underserved. The order also used terms such as "marginalized" and "adversely affected by persistent poverty and inequality." I may be wrong but that sounds like the admission of inherent institutional, systemic and constitutive inequality.

Another one of Biden's effort to extend equal rights was to extend federal nondiscrimination protections to members of the LGBTQ community. This order actually complimented a Supreme Court decision that expanded protections against discrimination based on sex in federal agencies to include sexual orientation, gender identity. Take note, it addressed discrimination in federal agencies. Do federal agencies support and exemplify the rights of the citizens of the nation?

Another executive order directed by Biden was dealing with unequal housing policies. It was not to overturn an injustice, but to evaluate or examine the effects of an unfair Trump policy.

To be fair unequal housing policies existed from the arrival of the first settlers, continuing after slavery and throughout the rest of our existence. The Department of Housing and Urban Development was directed to review regulatory actions that undermined fair housing policies and laws. If the review or finding determined policies are in fact unfair they would be addressed.

I have added this next topic because someone told me that the Bible degrades and is intolerant to the LBGT community. That is incorrect. First homosexuality is denounced in the Old Testament. Christianity is based on Jesus Christ or the New Testament. Secondly it doesn't seem to apply for the priest who sodomize little boys. To be a Christian does not mean you have to invite every LGBQT to your birthday party. But does mean you treat them with respect, justly and with love. And contrarily you should not isolate or not invite specifically because of someone's sexual preference, color or religion. If you do not invite them it should be because their idiots, untrustworthy or racist.

Before I move on from inequality and equal rights, I want to discuss voting rights. What is the key driving component of a society being democratic? Free and fair elections? The right to vote? The right of all Americans to choose whom their representatives will be, to enact equal and unequal policies. Who would say preventing persons from voting is patriotic or democratic? I know many of those who support Trump would. They rely on the fact that it is being done legally. There we go again with the whole legal versus Christian thing. Again Biden's administration is attempting to prevent the decimation of voting rights. Question. Why does administration even have to protect people's rights in the self proclaimed greatest Christian democracy in the world?

I almost forgot to discuss education or the lack of quality education for all. There are many factors that contribute to the inequality in the American education system. There are government policies, the placement of experienced teachers, lack of funding and lack of school supplies, to included books and technology. As with everything else this ties into inequality, poverty, the haves and have nots with terms such as systemic highlighted. I will discuss how the government had to enact laws to make education available. Then the inequality of affordable and equal educational opportunities and the false, deceptive educational curriculum.

Education policies have been drafted throughout the years, to address planning and set forth the principles for educating students. As we look at education policies, we see they are as convoluted as all the other policies and have had the same lingering affect. Educational policies have evolved as society and culture have changed throughout America's history. Like many policies and bills they are continually being debated and amended. Like many other democratic advantages of social mobility our country's ranking in the world of education has been steadily declining. What has America's policies been on education? Well, since we should all know the past, I will re-educate everyone.

Teaching others began during Biblical times. Children were typically educated in the skills in which they needed to sustain a standard of living. Individual families taught their children as they saw fit. The only group setting done was at temples in order to teach children the politics and practices of the nations or sects religion. This practice was pretty much adopted by the early colonies. It is in the New Old World that we again see the distinction between public and private. In colonial times education was primarily private and religious. Most children learned to read in order to study the Bible and the new laws of the settlements. This was actually the first law regarding education enacted by the Massachusetts General Court in 1642, but not all parents complied. In 1647 another Massachusetts Law, the Old Deluder Satan Act, was put in place. This was to require that a schoolmaster would be hired who would teach children to read and write in all towns of over fifty families. Then laws were adopted for towns of a hundred families to prepare children to attend Harvard College. The first government-owned and operated public high school, Boston Latin School, was founded in 1635.

Flipping back to Biblical education requirements. I hope everyone understands that this did not help America become

Christian but actually diluted the teaching of Jesus and propagated false teachings of man's own view point, of what they wanted students to become, believe and follow. Why do I say that? Two main reasons. One. Less than scholarly individuals taught the Bible to students. As a matter of fact prior to specific private Christian schools children learned from the perspective of those whom themselves were not yet ready to receive the fruits. Two, if children were taught the teachings of Jesus, there would never have been the inequalities and desolation of cultures and races. As America established its independence and became a sovereign nation, the call for public education grew. But there was still inequities in the newly formed education system. Very few students from poor families, American Indians, or African Americans were educated and girls were still educated at home. Quakers, when able, established charity schools to serve these under-represented groups. During the next century public school education grew. States became responsible for overseeing their respective education systems. But universal inequality became legal when in1896 the U.S. Supreme Court case, Plessy v. Ferguson, legalized segregation in "separate but equal" schools. This resulted in states having different requirements and providing education to those they chose. So, where are we now?

Good news. In 1954 Plessey vs. Ferguson was overruled by the Supreme Court in the Brown v. Board of Education decision that outlawed segregation in spite of the objections from most in the country. Ten years later Title VI of the Civil Rights Act prohibited discrimination based on race, color or national origin in public schools. Why was there still a need to have to formally institute a Civil Rights Act? Remember centuries long practices of not respecting God's word, and the Constitution I might add, meant the court's decision still would not undo our countries inequality in education. Throughout the next few decades many policies were instituted to assist aid to schools in poor rural and urban areas, federal aid for poor postsecondary students and acts against discrimination based on sex and disabilities. As in all policies, there were loopholes and special considerations. In

1980 Congress officially formed The Department of Education. This was an effort to standardize and enforce the previous acts empowered to the states. Was this an hooray moment? Not really. Our country would not provide education, and freedom" to many without being forced by the courts.

Now that the Supreme Court ruled everyone should have the right to education, what did the leaders and unGodly constituents of our beloved country put into place. With all the policies put in place as an attempt to either help the less fortunate or to give the illusion of helping, why is there is still inequality in the education system? A few reasons. For centuries those educated were actually those coming from the most educated families. Education became much like land and healthcare. Private versus public and sold to the highest bidder. My mind races at the injustice committed against those whom wanted the simple chance to have a good education. Even today tenured teachers go to the best white or economically supported schools. The less experienced teachers start at the worst schools, in the worst neighborhoods, with the least supplies and support. Is this an accident of by chance? No. It is institutional. And because of it, the United States lags far behind other countries when ranking education. I'll save this for last and now discuss what is taught.

As Christians, our responsibilities are to make sure that we and our children are educated in the most godly manner possible. And no, I am not saying everyone should go to Christian schools. Negative. We should not let a school board, school departments and educators teach our children ungodly philosophies. By ungodly I am not talking about anything in opposition to the Bible. I am talking about historical untruths for the sake of continuing a false sense of self and world views. I am talking about untruths by omission, that paint a false picture. God has entrusted us with children, and He will want an accounting of what we did with them. This said, my point is that both Christian and non-secular schools should do one thing. Teach the truth. The whole truth and nothing but the truth. That truth applies to a curriculum taught to everyone regardless of race, creed or economic status. There should be no hidden agendas, no serving the children Kool-Aid to drink.

In the 1947 Supreme Court decision of Everson v. Board of Education, Justice Wiley Rutledge argued that the religious clause in the Constitution's First Amendment actually resulted in the defining of history. He also argued that to argue that the Founders intended the First Amendment to create a strict separation of church and state. When the Founding fathers decided there should be separation of church and state they made sure all had the power to frame or alter education lessons based on the Christian view. In 2010, the Texas State Board of Education voted to scrub public school textbooks of anything that spoke of or mentioned any 'pro-Islam' or 'anti- Christian bias. In the year 2010! In other words, public schools would now be required to use school curriculums that whitewash Christians and demonize Muslims. Though relatively new to public education, Islamophobia has long run rampant at Christian schools. If it was based on the truth I would have no problem..

In conservative Christian schools, historical events are filtered through the literal Biblical creation story, and can be understood in the context of sin, redemption and "God's plan" for the United States. A certain school curriculum opens with a full-on endorsement of theocracy, stating, "All governments are ordained by God, but none compare to government by God.." From there, the curriculum pushes the false belief that the United States was founded as a Christian nation. And I do not mean subjectively or in theory or attempted to, I mean some are taught that the reason colonist came to America was to freely practice and growth Christianity. That is false teaching. At least tell the whole story. This curriculum also taught that horses would not exist in the USA, if Christians did not bring them from Europe.

The racist history of the United States is usually white washed or romanticized in Christian school curriculum. Bob Jones has eluded that "To help them endure the difficulties of slavery, God gave Christian slaves the ability to combine the African heritage of song with the dignity of Christian praise. Through the Negro spiritual, the slaves developed the patience to wait on the Lord and discovered that the truest freedom is from the bondage of sin." Another Christian textbook says, "A few slave holders were undeniably cruel. Examples of slaves beaten to death were not common, neither were they unknown. The majority of slave holders treated their slaves well." Even the Klan gets whitewashed. A Bob Jones textbook states that "the Klan in some areas of the country tried to be a means of reform, fighting the decline in morality and using the symbol of the cross to target bootleggers, wife beaters and immoral movies."

Many Christian schools teach young earth Christian creationism, that is, the idea that God literally created the earth, humans and animals in seven days, all of 4,000 years ago, in lieu of learning about the science of the Man's existence. Another book states that its, "Science and Health Program presents the universe as the direct creation of God and refutes the man-made idea of evolution." It is one thing to tell both sides, refute one, but do not tell one view point as an indoctrination or conditioning. Using Christian textbooks the curriculum taught many bias untruths. While working at a Christian school I was personally told that the genocide of Native Americans was justified because they were heathens as I previously mentioned. I would surmise that a majority of our proud conservative Christians believe that today.

That is enough about the curriculum. But what about the structure of education, the advancements of the greatest Christian nation on Earth. Or the growing decline of affordable educational resources. But what about the nation as a whole. Is it by accident the wealthy, higher tax bracket dwelling students get the best education. The best teachers, books, technology and even field trips. Is it an accident that poverty directly effects one's educational opportunities. Shouldn't the philosophy of Christian schools be to ensure all God's children are educated? Without an agenda.

Now, why are public inner, city and rural schools consistently producing lower test scores and a higher dropout rate? Is it because inner city children are less intelligent or because inner city children have less resources to learn. A few quick points before I move on.

Schools are funded based on the tax base, not the need. That in itself cause a systemic endless cycle of lack, being behind and continually living with the understanding that your situation does not deserve the same attention and respect as someone of wealth. This means everything from books to supplies are either hand me downs, cheap or ghost. The lack of funding means when the rest of the world is adapting to new technology and learning things that will carry them into the future, children from the inner city or rural areas can only learn from their outdated books, from their inexperienced teachers.

Experienced teachers with a good track record get to choose the schools they teach at. This means inner city schools are historically full of new, inexperienced teachers. Teacher, unless from the innercity cannot relate to or help the children overcome social barriers.

Many forms of discrimination are still prevalent in the American education system. From slavery to Jim Crow. From the industrial revolution to the Depression. From institutional biases and prejudices. How do we move towards being a more civilized and humane society? It begins with teaching, showing and living by example. There are too many examples of legal avenues in which inequality can flourish and even go unnoticed. But I submit the argument that if we go back and look at what Jesus taught, what the past empires did, what our forefathers tried to prevent and on what our country based its socio-economic system we should clearly see inequality was always prevalent. Inequality is the underlying cause of the following social ills we will discuss.

We will now talk about poverty related policies. Not the actual poor but the state of poverty in the United States and the policies that were designed to end poverty or adversely ensured it flourishes. When we look at poverty we are focusing on the systematic root causes of the collective poor. Where do I begin? Remember we are now focusing on our nation as it is today. I will focus on the policies of many politicians and citizens that have enabled and supported the behaviors I am about to dive into.

Since President Johnson's speech in 1964, where he vowed (not really) "not only to relieve the symptom of poverty, but to cure it and, above all, to prevent it", there have been many policies to assist the poor or less fortunate with food and living expenses. It was called the "War on Poverty". It was determined that those earning less than three times their annual budget for food would be considered poor and eligible for public assistance. Unfortunately, none of the many programs have cured or prevented poverty. Let me give an overview of the policies enacted throughout the years. It should go without saying that many of the following policies are always up for debate, depending what side of the bed the country got up on.

In 1964 The Economic Opportunity Act was adopted. The act created the Office of Economic Opportunity (OEO), which provided funds for vocational training and created Job Corps. During the next few decades the following programs were enacted. Early childhood education programs, the Earned Income Tax Credit, Nutrition assistance programs, Housing assistance program, Medicaid and the Children's Health Insurance Program (CHIP) and Cash assistance programs. Food stamps or now the Supplemental Nutrition Assistance Program (SNAP), Welfare or Temporary Assistance for Needy Families (TANF), school lunch programs and housing assistance such as Section Eight all assist the less fortunate. For those who have never read a book these programs are exclusive of race or gender. These policies included Supplemental Security Income (SSI) which offered aid to qualifying elderly and disabled. Food Stamps which gave low-income people coupons to purchase food. This became the SNAP initiative. The Earned Income Tax Credit (EITC) supply limited refunds of a family's social security taxes. Public Housing program subsidized dwellings for low-income families. Rent

Vouchers provided grants to low-income individuals to help housing costs. Medicaid, which we will discuss later provided low-cost medical care to those on welfare. But it has been argued that these programs are against the so- called American principles. I ask those who say those things, "Is helping the less fortunate really in opposition to American ideology"? I will definitely discuss that thinking later. All these policies definitely helped the poor. The policies definitely helped those who were able to utilize them. But for many, of all races, these policies ensured they could survive while remaining in the impoverished condition. There were no policies to end poverty, just to ensure it did not get out of hand. I will admit that some of the administrations whom enacted these policies had their heart in the right place. I will introduce the argument that some of these programs were not designed to end poverty, but to ensure its continuance. Also some politicians from a particular party have tried their best to end policies assisting the poor. Note - Biden's ordered an executive order expanding food assistance programs. This program was to extend the increase in Supplemental Nutrition Assistance Program benefits and allow states to increase SNAP emergency allotments. It also intended to increase benefits under another aid program, the Pandemic Electronic Benefits Transfer, which gives students money for food.

Everyone should be able to take advantage of the same policies that ensure the rich get richer. Things like subsidies, tax loopholes and the chance to take advantage of those things. Unfortunately those living in poverty cannot. Politicians introducing subsidies and tax loopholes have created billions of dollars for corporations and the super wealthy. I am not against opportunity but according to the Bible and the Constitution those opportunities should be freely given to every man, woman and child. Irrespective of race, creed, ethnicity or social background. Anyone with enough intelligence should realize this. Since then several policies were put in place to assist a certain demographic. I guess many are pondering. Well, if there were so many policies to prevent poverty, what happened? That is where we go back and have to understand words like institutionalize and systemic. Also, we have to realize poverty is an inherent system developed and cultivated for centuries. Make that millenniums.

Trump proposed changes that would alter the way the government determines which families are impoverished, a move that would cut millions of Americans off from benefits such as Medicaid, housing assistance, and food stamps.

He also proposed rules that would cause over 3 million Americans to lose food assistance benefits, and make more than 500,000 kids ineligible for free school meals. The administration has also tried to impose new work requirements on health care, public housing, and housing subsidies.

The Trump administration has previously proposed drastic cuts to after-school programs for poor families, and a grant program that helps train teachers and reduce class sizes. It also proposed capping the amount of money students and families can borrow for post-secondary schooling, a measure that would make it harder for working-class families to compete with their richer peers for schooling.

In a losing effort Trump's administration repeatedly attempted to repeal the Affordable Care Act, which would have forced millions Americans to lose health coverage.

Meanwhile, under Trump the Department of Housing and Urban Development proposed a rule that would deny federal housing aid to undocumented immigrants and anyone living with people residing in the country illegally. His administration's Department of Justice examined how it can weaken civil rights rules that prevent discrimination in housing and education. Such rules bans housing industries, housing lenders, and landlords from creating policies that negatively impact a particular minority group if there are other means of achieving what those policies set out to do, in a less discriminatory way. His administration crippled an Obama-era rule called Affirmatively Furthering Fair Housing (AFFH), which is intended to better enforce the Fair Housing Act and combat housing discrimination, a problem that has persisted throughout the country. Trump also proposed cuts would cut other programs, like job training. We must understand that poverty rate stems from politics, not economics. He is not President so some could say it is a moot point. My point is he would never had done it if the country as a whole stood for equality. That is why there is a constant partisan battle to keep this small advantages. For those who argue that programs do not help because of family dynamics or because of parents are lazy and not working, I submit this. The destruction of the nuclear family, the proliferation of the single parent household, and the grandparent household has led to the unraveling of many programs and generations. I would say on purpose. To tell a single parent they cannot get assistance unless they earn a certain wage but systematically restrict ones opportunity to earn a decent wage is, evil. Yes, evil. Many work driven policies hurt working families with children. Especially those who need child care, insurance and support. Well, all that said let's talk about how policies where otherwise revised. As a reminder.

Blessed are you who are poor, for yours is the kingdom of God.

Blessed are you who hunger now, for you will be satisfied. Luke 6:20-21 NIV

How has our country's obvious Holy Spirit, Fruits of the Spirit filled, Christian policy having nation done over the years with poverty. How does America rank globally as far as poverty? Now we can look at it many ways. One, based on population, GDP or wealth, or even amongst other predominantly Christian nations. Poverty might mean different things in different parts of the world and to different people, but it is largely defined as being unable to afford a minimum standard of living. The United States has come a long way in addressing the problem, but progress seems to have slowed despite the recent years of economic recovery. Again I ask, 'Who did the economic recovery benefit?"

Poverty is caused by institutional policies put in place over many years. This is separate from just helping the poor, but focuses more on the socio- economic causes of poverty. There are a lot of things we can discuss. The ranking of impoverished populations in this great country. The number of Americans living in poverty and their demographics. Maybe we can discuss the contributing factors of those impoverished. I am sure you know we will discuss a little bit of everything. And of course how poverty affects one's ability to afford healthcare in today's Christian-Capital system. We can discuss the job market and its social limitations. Though the economy has added millions of jobs, many of the jobs created are not the same as jobs that were lost. In many areas, the problem of poverty has worsened during the recovery. I am grateful to those Christians and all people who live in service of others. But, in many ways, the problem has even escalated. Poverty is perhaps the most persistent of problems, with consequences that can span a lifetime, be transferred across generations, and loom in the minds of individuals and families living at the edge of poverty.

How do you think many American Christians view poverty. Surprisingly many far right Christian thinkers tend to more often blame a pure lack of effort as the cause of poverty. I guess they do not understand that poverty can result from difficult circumstances beyond ones control.

Something equally as important as our view of poverty is how the world views America's ranking of and addressing poverty.

In short, most Americans, whom by the way or not poor, believe poverty is caused by lack of effort, complacency and the desire for one to remain in poverty. Most of many countries around the world feel a little different. Though they may believe in the complacency of the poor, they acknowledge that developed countries with great numbers living in poverty have institutional systems which are designed to uphold the status quo of the haves and have nots.

Although the US has a long history of prosperity, mobility, and justice, too many people have been left behind, struggling to get by, with little hope for a better future. Fifty million Americans live on incomes below the federal poverty level, including one in every four children. Poverty is not a good thing for our country, politically, nationally globally, or religiously. Poverty is about power, not scarcity. The richest country in the world should be able to sustain an economy that is healthy and fair. People who are willing and able to work at a full-time job should be able to earn enough money to support their families and have opportunities to climb the ladder out of poverty. The greatest Christian nation should not give poverty wages based on a capitalist ideology. Millions of people today work in jobs that pay poverty level low wages, provide few or no benefits and mandate persons work irregular schedules. Some profit driven companies, owned by church going people, force their workers to work in unsafe conditions. When employees attempt to speak out and stand up for their rights they are reprimanded or even fired. In essence, these workers are denied the basic right to "decent work." Not coincidentally, they are also among those who have historically had to struggle for their rights. These people are working harder and longer than ever, falling behind, and losing hope. As our economy widens the gap, our democracy falters.

Let me transition to the wealthy and our glowing world recognized economy. What led to the growth of our magnanimous economy. In order to understand the structure of our economy you must go back to what made it the strongest economy in the world. Was it innovation or was it superior intellect? Was it God and the greatness of our divine worship and praise? Maybe it was slavery, low wages, pillaging and war. In short, there were many things fueled by the laws and policies that allowed the rich to get richer and the rest of the country to help the rich flourish. From tax holes, loops and incentives, grants, contracts and favors, and a population to provide the labor. We all know the statistics about the ratio of the wealthy, super wealthy, the so-called middle class and the poor. Again, I am not a communist. I am a capitalist, though hanging on to the middle class ladder. Yet I still hope I hit the lottery for millions or be able to leave a fortune to my children. Through a life of vast experiences I now know, that the bigger picture for the success of mankind leans on humanity, kindness and everyone at least having an equal chance as everyone else. My vast experiences is a story for another time. Back to the wealthy. Again, let be qualify my statements. There is nothing wrong with being wealthy. Being wealthy, greedy, dishonest and selfish is a problem. There is a percentage of people who have obtained wealth through his or her hard work. Sports and the entertainment industries are responsible for many of them. Nightly practice and grinding. There are also those who came from lower income or single parent families and were the first to go to college. The ones who became doctors, lawyers, inventors, politicians and business persons. These are the exception. Let me state, it is not the duty of the wealthy to divide their money equally amongst the have-nots. I do somewhat believe in Matthew 22:20-22. "Render therefore unto Caesar the things which are Caesar's; and unto God the things that are God's" I believe helping the country as a whole just by paying taxes is not a bad idea. I believe forcing the less fortunate to pay higher taxes is spiritually and morally wrong and should be illegal. I also feel having those who worked to make someone else's fortune to wind up homeless or destitute is a sin. That said I appreciate those of means that will give to those less fortunate. I am not talking about the rich who periodically donate taxable funds to a charity.

In spite of any doctrine that prosperity is for all and financial status is the result of personal merit, poverty extends to practically all aspects of U.S. society. Despite the many anti-poverty policies, it remains largely unaddressed. Why would it remain unaddressed in a powerful Christian nation? It is also relatively undiscussed in public discourse and incompletely understood by the public and academics alike. One thing I would like to point out. That the political right would like us to believe that programs to help the poor are not Christian but Socialist. Maybe they are not Christian or Socialist. Maybe they are just caring human beings.

If Jesus believed that belief is about action, why do not we? Why have we not dedicated ourselves to bringing true discipleship and love to others, when it is what Christ told us to do? God has asked us to demonstrate our belief by bringing good news to those who feel hopeless. We are called to drop everything for Him and take the chance to do what is right and just. Jesus envisions what the world could look like and calls us to join God in the process of making that vision a reality. What good is belief without it offering true hope? Hope is what the country and the world needs. As time progressed the rapid growth of sinful nations led to the poverty of the common person. But the currency of Jesus' kingdom is different than ours. Jesus' economy or riches was based on self-sacrifice and His currency was the love and service to all. For Jesus, belief and actions are one and in the same. You have to live a life with other people in mind and you have to give freely. You cannot have one without the other. Oh, I guess if we applied that principle, would we still be a capitalist Christian country. Or would we just be Socialist?

Now let's run through healthcare policies. Poverty and wealth pay an important part in how our healthcare system operates. From care to cost to profit. The United States has the most expensive healthcare system on earth. We spend billions more on healthcare than other industrialized nations. Trillions are spent on healthcare annually. In spite of all the spending, the government subsidies, tax breaks, grants and contracts given to pharmaceutical companies and insurance conglomerates, we are ranked 37th in the world among developed countries. Patient care, employee health, drug development and distribution, patient information handling and even administrative policies. There are also several policies resulting in our low ranking and causes the spiral of Americans Christian or not, to unnecessarily lose their life. What are some of those related policies or economic structures?

There are many healthcare related policies. Healthcare policies determine the cost one must pay for care, the access one has to care, the quality of care received and ultimately whether or one receives the best healthcare available, the worst healthcare or none at all. The United States has a public and private system which is run by what is called a third-party payer system. That means a health insurance plan reimburses doctors for the bulk of the cost of healthcare services provided to patients. Most Americans are enrolled in private health insurance through their employer.

The remainder have public insurance. The private insurance system jacks up the price of healthcare causing obscene overpricing.

The two major public programs are Medicaid and Medicare. Medicaid became into practice as result of President Johnson's legislation in 1965 and was designed to provide health coverage for low-income people. Today, Medicaid provides coverage for over 70-million American citizens and reimburses hospitals for almost 50-percent of all medical expenses It also included a provision to provide insurance for low-income individuals. Medicare is for people 65 years and older. It also covers younger people with certain disabilities or kidney disease who are of cause not low-income. Other major policies include the Children's Health Insurance Program (CHIP), the Hospital Readmissions Reduction Program (HRRP), the Patient Safety and Quality Improvement Act (PSQIA) and of course the Affordable Care Act. Now many people are already yelling, so what is the problem? But what I am not listing is the multitude of policies that allow healthcare providers and pharmaceutical companies to make as much profit as legally allowed. There is also the fact that the best hospitals, doctors and overall healthcare exist in neighborhoods that are more privileged. Just like the better the neighborhood, the better the schools, grocery stores and quality of life. Well that's the overview. I forgot one more thing. Healthcare coupled with greed has enabled the production and flooding of harmful and even deadly drugs. I guess I can discuss that when I talk about crime.

Many of these policies directly result in our country not honoring its duty to ensure the right to healthcare, whether decent or not. The right to live in a safe neighborhood, the right to receive healthcare is all tied to one thing. Money. It is this premise that goes against the humanity of Christianity and sprouts into the other damaging factors. It is not about not having God's favor or not applying oneself. My answer, read the Bible. Our healthcare system was designed as almost everything else in America. It is a commodity, a for-profit institution. It is not an equal right for all. Is having a car an equal right for all? No, because it is a commodity. Is having healthcare an equal right for all? No, because it is a commodity. For those who do not know what a commodity is, let me explain. The short explanation is a commodity is a good that can be bought and sold. It had historically been associated with things you would go shopping for such as cars, fruit, gold and toilet tissue. The definition is a little broader in this aspect. It can be extended to anything of value. Legal representation, education and even drinking clean water. Since healthcare is a commodity, it is sold. It is a for- profit system. The fact that it is for-profit allows for crazy high pricing. This includes private insurance and drug cost. Not everyone can equally afford.

Does our great country's policies and desire to be a shining example of the fruits of Christianity compare to how we care for our sick, wounded and impaired? First, let me run the statistics by everyone. Taken into count America's greatness at being democratic, an industrial super-power and Christian one would think our healthcare system and the overall health of its citizens rank the highest in the world. Contrarily, the United States spends the most on healthcare but ranks near the bottom of the pile amongst industrialized, Christian nations. Over fifty million Americans do not have adequate access to healthcare. We are also the only industrialized country in the world where people die from no healthcare and the only one that does not provide some type of universal health coverage. My take is most who feel healthcare is not a responsibility of Christians or not the responsibility of the government usually argues that if we task the government with providing healthcare we would be adopting socialist ideologies. I will discuss this ignorant thinking later. My take is that Christians are called to, and even required to pursue equitable health care for everyone regardless of any sacrifice and especially if the limit of such is financial. Christians are called to pursue the welfare of the city by seeking social justice and caring for the sick. Look at the Books of Jeremiah, Micah and Matthew to name a few. Other nations also look at America as a country that does not care for the welfare of its citizens, not alone the citizens of other countries.

One troubling fact is that America has the resources to provide everyone in this country health care, but the topic has become so politicized that we are conditioned to believe that saving lives and preventing disease is a partisan issue. It is a partisan issue that, stems from a capitalist issue. If it were a moral issue or spiritual issue then partisanship would not be a factor. Research continues to show that as citizens gain better coverage and access to health services, their health outcomes improve. The decision should be Jesus based. The gravity of these implications cannot be trivialized and must lead the Christian to action. The Christian must step away from their political allegiance and stand for a health system where all citizens can receive equitable health care. However, as with all morally good endeavors, it comes at a cost. Christians are called to bear one another's burdens. For Christians who think that lack of healthcare is a self-inflicted condition or due to lack of prayer, what about cancer, critical injuries, genetic diseases and even sports related injuries. I have read articles written by Christians who claim they should just try prayer, cloth wraps and oils. Is this coming from Biblical text or just an excuse or in some cases a scam.

Now, everyone, Christian or not should be able to afford or have the right to healthcare. The fact there is not free healthcare and the fact that there are Americans who cannot afford health insurance itself is horrendous, inequitable, and un-Christian. Healing was one of the main points and miracles in the Bible. Whom did Jesus heal? The Pharisees? No. The rich? No. He healed those whom did not have the care afforded to the rich. Because someone cannot afford medical care does not mean they should be denied the God given right to live. Especially because a service provider will only make 50 billion instead of 51 billion. It means that someone who can't afford insurance does not die because of an injury or because of an infection that $10 antibiotics could have prevented, because the pharmaceutical company is charging $300. Some studies show that a significant portion of personal bankruptcies are due to medical expenses. Sixty-two percent of all American bankruptcies are due to unpaid medical bills; seventy-eight percent of these families were insured at the time.

While part of the solution is to fix the massive cost of health, another part is to prevent financial ruin from an unforeseen health event. This means that hard-working people should not need to choose between a life-saving treatment, their children's college funds and sometimes even their marriage. It also means that there is a greater chance of contracting a life threatening illness if you are impoverished or now even middle class. So, the cycle is constant. Poverty, poor health, sub standard education, crime so on and then the next generation is born to repeat the cycle. Ok I got off point! Back to healthcare.

To develop a system that protects everyone, all must be willing to bear some financial burden. This is where people squirm. No one likes making less money for something they might never use. The leading train-of-thought among many health professionals is that if all Americans were to buy-in to health insurance, the cumulative pool of money would sufficiently cover the country's medical expenses. For the Christian who pays more than they utilize, they are faced with a question that reveals their heart. Was my money wasted because I did not benefit personally or was it well-invested because it helped others?

Now there were policies like the Affordable Care Act which intended to provide health coverage to those who could not afford private insurance and did not qualify for public assistance. Was ObamaCare totally equitable or without flaws? No. But it was an attempt. It was done in good faith, with faith. Policies in which Trump tried to overturn. Not because of his uncanny love for the Bible, but because so many uneducated people claim that makes us socialist. Many things Jesus taught was based on future socialist ideology. That is another conversation for another day.

In an effort to counter Trump's attempts to strike down the Affordable Care Act, Biden signed an order directing agencies to re-examine policies that undermined protections for people with pre-existing conditions, complicated the process of enrolling in Medicaid and the Affordable Care Act and reduced coverage and affordability of the programs. Am I saying Biden did that because he is a Christian? Not at all, I have no idea of his reasons. Maybe he just knew it was the right thing to do.

Another issue to evaluate is how we treat mental illness. It is hard to objectively measure mental health conditions. This is because so many institutions, medical professionals and governments use different criteria for defining or measuring mental health. What about an unarmed innocent man with mental illness being shot and killed? I submit that the person shooting the innocent person, must suffer from a mental illness.

I look at the issue of mental health from a cause and effect view. What are the causes of mental health issues? I start by easily characterizing two main causes. One is medical, neurological, DNA, some internal problem one is born with and will exist no matter of his or her circumstance. The other is caused by life. Heartbreaks, despair, loss of loved ones or status, and the overall stress of life. We have normally associated and treated the former with more concerning yet drastic measures. We have recently begun to acknowledge the latter. However, we have not yet figured out how to treat or assist beyond support groups or an occasional prescription. Has societal caused mental illness always existed? Or has is it drastically increased in the past few decades. Mental illness is defined using a wide range of mental health conditions. These disorders affect one's mood, thinking and behavior. The five most common mental health disorders include depression, anxiety, eating disorders, substance abuse and attention deficit disorder. Then there is of course plain insanity. Common signs of mental illness in adults and adolescents can include excessive worrying or fear and feeling excessively sad or low. According to those signs, I guess I sometime suffer from mental illness.

I am bringing up mental health for two reasons. The first is the fact that how mental health is diagnosed and more over treated, depends greatly on one's socio-economic status. Many low income persons do not even receive the acknowledgement, diagnosis or treatment as someone of capability or wealth. This ties into the whole equality and poverty issues previously raised. Just as many are destined to live poverty, many are destined to live their lives with mental health issues and behind the eight ball. Fact, one's economic status will determine whether or not they are shot dead for yielding a knife or asked to be careful entering a police car after shooting up a store or school. The second reason is that mental health has been used as an excuse for those committing violent acts against others and those using one's health issue as a justification for their murder. I personally feel anyone who kills innocent people by bombs or shooting must have something wrong with their heads. They are all cuckoo if you ask me. I also feel anyone shooting an unarmed person with a mental health issue is sinful and has no religion. Or I guess they can just be scared chicken.. you know. Those committing mass murders no matter the reason or the underlying causes are all terrorist, though most in America disagree.

There have been more articles written which examined the mental health of terrorist than that of Christians. But the terrorist studied were Muslim. So stating the results of that study would be counterproductive or just a moot point. But there are the statistic on terrorists who claim Christian motivation. Please note, I am staying on task so using the definition of terrorism, I will discuss in regards to people committing terrorist acts whom claim to be Christian. Just to note. They could have been characterized as socially awkward or isolated. People in terrorist groups are also less likely to have a mental illness than the general population, possibly due to the selection criteria of such groups.

Mental illness does not seem to unduly prevent terrorists from performing successful complex attacks.

We will discuss more about mass shooters and terrorists when we speak about crime in America.

Fundamentalist Christian ideology has been the inspiration for terrorism and figures like radio host, news anchors and politicians are damaging America by helping 'promote vengeance seeking'. I believe those who listen to this insanity all have mental health issues. You never notice the person stirring the pot ever acting on what they preach. I will also state that any radical ideology that promotes terrorism or an eye for and eye should reconsider his or her commitment to Christian practices. It could be just the fight fire with fire mentality. Yes that could be justified in the scriptures. But we have to consider the Testament, books and scriptures of those sections of the bible, where stories or history is telling the story where God's children were given the mercy to act vengeful. But even in those cases, they were life and death. Usually the last stand. Not because a person was mad or thought, too many diverse cultures were moving into certain neighborhoods or holding certain jobs. I believe that now we are mindful of the out of date scripture and even use it to justify harsh acts. Nowadays we commit harsh acts just be cause. Because we falsely comprehend the bible or just think that being a Christian gives one the right to commit harsh acts.

Another view point is just that the people who commit violent terrorist acts as defined, are clearly mentally ill.

Now let us switch to crime. The causes of and types of crime have been discussed, analyzed and debated, in thousands of political science, law, psychology, social science and medical books. So, I will try to keep it as brief as possible. First let me ask, what is crime? Or better yet, how do each of you define or classify crime? Is it a legal thing or is it a humanity thing? Well, we will revisit that later. What are our policies on crime? Maybe a better question would be, what are our policies for crime prevention? Are there clear universal prevention policies?

When discussing crime policies, it is important to understand the difference between "crime deterrence", "crime control and crime prevention". Crime prevention policies are designed to reduce, if not, stop crime. The word prevention is somewhat misdirected. Crime control policies were developed to maintain an approved level of crime. To control crime. Approved or appropriate, who decides? What is the deciding factor or even the equation? We can also use the term "crime deterrence" Policies have been instituted to deter felonies, such as the three strikes law, which basically aims just to scare the repeat offender. Policies have been enacted to deter minorities by instituting unreasonable or unequitable sentencing. Whatever definition you may think is appropriate we will see that certain crimes have been part of the fabric of who our country is since its inception. Yes, crime has existed throughout time, but we are talking about our great US of A. To eliminate pages of subjectivity and further debate, I won't discuss all the crimes committed prior to the Constitution and the adoption of man's laws.

As previously mentioned, policies and laws are created at different levels of government. Public polices at the state level with even more independent or "micro" policies at the local level. Criminal related policies are created at the federal level and state criminal policies and laws. This can and has caused much inconsistencies and inequalities. We know there are great biased legal recourses and punishments.

There is another take on policies that have an effect on crime. Those are the policies that may actually lead to crime or those acts which cause, nurture and even support the inherent conditions that may lead to crime. Human rights policies, foreign policies, individual state policies and inequitable "status quo" policies, have not prevented crime, but helped it nurture. I could cite hundreds of examples or sum them all up by stating, "crimes where the laws have been circumvented" or crimes where the laws were intended to provide shelter or one class and the incarceration of another class. Again, we see that sometimes preventing or convicting perpetrators of crime has always been somewhat unequal. As a Christian nation how does our country view or address crime? We will begin discussing crime in general.

Back to the question. What is crime? How is crime defined? Is it a legal, constitutional definition or a moral definition? Webster may define crime as an action or omission that constitutes an offense that may be prosecuted by the state and is punishable by law. If crime is an offense punishable by law then someone who has committed a crime but, was not convicted is still technically a criminal. Synonymously crime may be defined as an action or activity that, although not illegal, is considered to be evil, shameful, or wrong. Many readers, Christians and politicians waiver or take advantage of the definition as appropriate. If it is not against a written law then for that time it is okay to perform the specific act. Such as apartheid when legal, such as slavery when legal, such as lynching when legal, such as marijuana when of course illegal. Then of course the self-righteous who believe if you don't get caught or "beat the rap", you never committed a crime. So how do you define what is a crime? Depending on how you answer that question will determine how you view the following text. Is sinning a crime? Unfortunately just about everyone would vote and emphatic no. However, their lives would reveal a great hypocrisy. A passage in 1 John 3:4 (ESV) of the New Testament does state, 'Everyone who makes a practice of sinning also practices lawlessness; sin is lawless'. Is lawlessness a crime? Based on that statement sinning is a crime. Have we instituted policies based on sinning? Of course not! Not only would that be outrageously complicated, it would also be impossible to qualify. Well it would be easy to qualify in a Christian society. There has never been a consensus on what a sin actually is even among Christians. And so, our dilemma sprouts its wings.

The great Christian United States leads in just about every crime related statistics, among so-called developed Christian nations. Gun related crimes, violent crimes, child sexual abuse, drug related crimes and corporate or political related crimes.

The overall crime situation should not be a partisan issue or debate. Take note that I omitted one of the most sinful and quasi-illegal crimes. Hate crimes. I will also note that in America, the self-professed, "far right" Christians usually commit hate crimes. Not Jews, not Muslims, not minorities. What do I mean by hate? Easy, crime committed where their cause can be directly to the victim being of a different race, ethnicity, religion or gender and attributed to a Christian philosophy or justification. Is that technically more heinous, illegal or immoral? It depends if we are addressing crime or sin. If you profess to be a Christian, you should know how much of the Bile speaks of hatred how it is a greater hypocritical offense and how it will be judged.

Before I get into the mass shootings, police shootings, lynching, and drugs let me mention a growing statistic. Faith-based fraud has grown to a least $35 billion annually. "Faith-based" fraud. It almost sounds like an oxymoron! It has actually become a specific category of crime and charges. In recent years, a significant number of pastors and parishioners have been involved in more crimes that have been exposed. These crimes consist of sexual abuse and fraud. That could be a result of news and social media. It could be that someone grew a conscious.

Now let us look at what policies have had an effect on defining crime, the rise of crime and the possible mitigation of crime. Policies that have reduced crime have been geared at inner cities and involve more policing. Actually community based organizations have made tremendous strides in cleaning up neighborhoods. Though policies have reduced inner city drugs, as a country we still almost solely fund drug cartels and drug imports. There are far more policies that helped crime flourish. Our international import laws, political agreements, socio-economic inequality and economic-political structures, such a capitalism and pharmaceuticals have led to inequalities resulting in a societal disaster. Laws and policies allowed for the surge of deadly legal prescription drugs. Addiction leads to crime. Easier put our countries policies creates and even emboldens crime.

How you may ask? Look at other countries that do not have a high crime rate. It is no doubt that the United States is one of global leaders in the world as far as crimes recorded and deaths caused by crime.

The United States has more fundamentalist Christians than any other nation. The United States also has a very high rate of violent crime, and particularly high rates of lethal violence, compared to other similarly situated nations. I should qualify that statistic and say the U.S. has a high rate of lethal violence, compared to other Christian nations. This is not a coincidence. This belief system, and the culture it inspires, lends itself to many types of criminal activity including the promotion of violent crimes against a variety of victims, terrorism against those of different faiths, and even crimes against the environment. We should also be aware of the obvious. Our country refuses to condemn guns, drugs, and anything that feeds into the economy. We have things like robbery, murder, thievery, bribery, extortion, rape, assault, tax evasion, various crimes against children and so much more. We can talk about drug violence or more exact, drug acceptance. Legal and illegal. There is also something many call victimless, consensual or false pretense crimes. We can discuss those later. It can be said that Christian fundamentalism has 'set the United States on a dangerous course' that is creating a tide of social problems, as well as an explosion of hate groups. Some may not agree with the term fundamentalist. Should I minimize the term to radical or insane? If posed with the question is the high crime rate due to the lack of Christianity or because of Christianity, what would your answer be? My answer would be based on a twist. The twist being the USA crime rate is so high because of the lack of Christianity and the lack of just good people. But my take on "the lack of Christianity" may surprise you. The lack of, isn't derived from people not professing to be Christian. However, contrary. The lack of Christians are dominated by those falsely professing to be Christians. You can profess anything, but then you can shoot and unarmed citizen in the back. You can profess anything, while holding a Bible, and squeeze the democracy, humanity and hope from the hearts and minds of millions. Okay. Let me get back on track.

I will just pick a few types of crimes. I will start with mass shootings. As I continue to add to this manuscript mass shootings continue occurring. So, let me cut to the chase. We know America leads most nations in mass shootings and resulting mass murders. Why does the greatest, Christian nation refuse to do anything to stop or minimally reduce this? There have been thousands of mass shootings in the US since Sandy Hook in 2013. In 2021, there were close to 700 persons killed and over two thousand injured. A mass or "active" shooting, is defined as an individual actively engaged in killing or attempting to kill people in a confined and populated area. Did a majority of those who committed mass shootings identify with Islam, Hinduism, Judaism or Christianity? Of course! Trick question. Those that profess to be a Christian. Lovers of God. Am I saying Christian's are bad? Not at all. Not real Christians. Don't get it twisted. I do think we need to examine what is taught and how we minister and provide support to one another. I also feel if someone professes that their country, religion or lifestyle is better than someone else, it should be manifested. The world should be able to witness our greatness beyond the number of billionaires. Besides mass shootings, our great country also leads all other developed and Christian nations in the killing of unarmed citizens, by of all people, law enforcement and in the killing of minorities and unarmed minorities. Has anyone heard about this!? Did you know that? Do gun toting Americans identify with the Constitution or Christianity. I guess if they are officers of the law, it must be the constitution. Most far right republicans, white supremist and radical idiots think the Constitution and the Bible are connected. Or then again do they really? I have seen billboards on interstate highways with an AR-15 and the slogan "To protect God and Country". Is their justification the Second Amendment or the teachings of Jesus? And the false interpretation of the Second Amendment at that! All I am asking is why, as a nation, we are not disgusted? Oh yeah money, lobbyist, the "trump" Jesus.

Why does the fatal trend of mass shooting prevail in God's country? Is it because our genius nation does not know how to stop the shootings? Is it because our great country puts money and lobbyist above the lives of their brethren? Well, I ask, is it because most of the persons have mental illness or because a great number of them are Christian zealots? Is there that big of a difference? Is there a cause an effect? Am I saying Christians are the cause or the reason mass shootings happen? Definitely not. I am saying the country's overall ideologies are to blame. I am saying Jesus and all His disciples and apostles were crucified for the right for us to live. And I personally feel if all the millions of Christians urged the politicians to do something, it could be addressed. Unfortunately the enablers of the crazy shooters claim to be loyal God fearing Americans. Maybe if the politicians were Christian or just humane and just they would lead the way on gun reform and mental illness. Over the last twenty years the number of hate groups have steadily increased. This goes to inequality and crime. I would also say mental illness! In 2008 with the election of Barack Obama as the first black president of the United States the number grew higher. When Donald Trump became president in 2016 and made his "demonizing", idiotic statements about Latinos and Muslims the radical right smelled themselves and the white nationalism sky-rocketed. The Ku Klux Klan has declined, while other white supremacist groups have substantially strengthened. Today there are hundreds of these radical hate groups. They include groups that are anti- Black, anti-Jew, anti-Muslim, anti- Gay, anti-immigrant (I guess those hate their own great grandparents), racist skin-heads, neo-Confederate, anti- woman, anti-Hispanic and neo-nazi. They are actually the scared punk version of the Nazis. And the new western world terrorist. Just about all not only identify with Christianity, but use it as a justification. So, I ask, "What makes a Christian?".

I am going to visit another issue. Terrorism. One where we will look at Christians who committed "terrorist" acts. And of course according to the definition of the word. My supposition is that someone who commits mass murder and claims religion is a terrorist. This applies to any religion and country including the USA whom coined the phrase. A terrorist can also be defined as a person who uses unlawful violence and intimidation, especially against civilians, in the pursuit of political aims. Now there a five types of terrorism as defined by agencies such as the FBI, the US DOD and the US DOS.

State-Sponsored terrorism, which consists of terrorist acts on a state or government by a state or government.

Dissent or domestic terrorism, which are terrorist groups which have rebelled against their government. Like the confederacy or even the January 6th schmucks. Terrorists and the Left and Right, which are groups rooted in political ideology.

Criminal Terrorism, which are terrorists acts used to aid in crime and criminal profit. An example would be the ransomware crew.

Religious terrorism, which are terrorist groups which are extremely religiously motivated. Now this would not apply to American citizens. Oh wait. Yes it would, when the rioters brought up God, Bibles and Jesus. When any person inflicting violence and hatred on others while blaspheming God's name. Religious terrorist can of course be Muslim, but unfortunately for those shouting that fact, this book isn't about Muslims or Islam.

Are terrorists who claim to have a Christian motivation can act alone or in groups, Christian terrorist?. It is often difficult to determine if the perpetrator acted completely alone or was inspired by a religious or political group. I know we coin a phrased "Islamic Terrorist" but is a Christian who shoots up a church or concert goers in Las Vegas "Christian Terrorist"? Are mass murderers who kill in the name of God or Christianity truly Christian? Are they terrorist? There are thousands in the past ten years, so I will tell of a few examples. I should also let you know that I consider mass murderers as terrorist.

Terrorist acts are things like walking into an abortion clinic armed with a a rifle and kerosene. Using door jams and home made mouth restraint and killing multiple persons. Terrorist acts include attacking Planned Parenthood locations, the Olympic grounds concerts, LGTBQ establishments, Jewish synagogues, and of course just random targets.

I could write another book just on the Christian extremist, zealot, terrorist. But I think you get the picture. Okay these men may have been extreme. There are hundreds of cases of bombings, shootings and lynching from the every day Joe. These mass murderers for some reason always identified with being a devout Christian as well as Aryan or identified with another radical and racist organization. Though claimed extremist views. I guess they were just Christian extremist.

Numerous individuals and groups have cited their Christianity or Christian beliefs as the motivation for their terrorist acts. And yes, so have those who claim to be Muslims, but we are talking about Christianity. Homegrown terrorists can cite their interpretation of the Bible or Christian beliefs as their motivation. For those who think I am just spewing on Christians. Not. In some cases terrorists may identify themselves as Christian, but not be motivated by any particular interpretation of Christian belief. The use of Christianity serves as a reason for violence and usually claims allegiance to a wider social group. In such cases Christianity is a label and does not necessarily have connection to any Christian, texts beliefs or practices. The perpetrator believes a particular group threatening, such as LGBT or any group that does not conform with the view they have of who they are. When the opposing group is also Christian but belongs to a different denomination, they are often denounced as non-Christian or anti-Christian.

Remember this when you label all Muslims as terrorist because they may identify with Islam. Maybe not all the crazy people I have discussed throughout this book are actually Christian. Maybe their profession was false. So what is a crime and what is a Christian?

Again let me be clear I am not calling Christians mass murderers or terrorist. I am stating without reservation that no true Christian is a mass murderer or terrorist. Just as no true Muslim would either. Though conventional Christian Bible interpretations also offer a number of sanctions against violence as a political or religious weapon. Will anyone ever rise up and preach the truth or was Jesus right on point telling us one of the most dangerous things in our times will be false prophets. As I move on, I want to touch on the selling of drugs. Every race, creed and economic groups sell drugs. Why? Because every one of the groups use drugs. The War on Drugs was much like the War on Crime. It did not stop the problem and it targeted lower income neighborhoods and minorities. To be fair there was a rise in homicides that needed to be addressed, but minorities were unjustly targeted. Facts show the selling of drugs to the surburban crowd fueled the policies to curtail drug sells.. Something said, but not really grasped, is the fact that if the United States government did not choose to support the importation of drugs in nthe first place, neighborhoods would never have been destroyed. Drugs were never produded in L.A, Chicago or New York. Drug paraphelia was not produced by inner city corporate giants. But our country turned a blind eye to ensure the inequality it depended on. Even educational system originally even taught that cocaine was not addictive.

The next topic is just down-right nasty, scary and decadent. Of the years there have been growing evidence and exposure of child molestation and pedophilia. The great USA has Boy Scout troop leaders, coaches and men of the dirty cloth molesting boys. I would call them homosexual, child molesting, pedophiles. Then we have the coaches and doctors molesting young girls. I would call them child-raping creeps. I have heard many try to justify their acts with the cover of mental illness. All I can say is they are crazy, but not legally mentally ill. And for all of them that stand up in a church, give communion, or use the term "Almighty God ", God is waiting for you. Trust that! Our whole, eco-political structure. In addition to, the lack of being able to teach and show universal love and respect. I have lived in another country that has legalized recreational drugs, nude beaches, a train system with no turnstiles, where paying is on the honor system and alcohol sold in gas stations amongst many other places. Believe it or not, that country has one of the lowest crime rates of All Democratic, Christian nations. Why? Go back and read.

Now as mentioned, there are the legal crimes. If you are asking how can a crime be legal, you haven't been paying attention or you just don't get it. I won't spend much time on this. There are probably more of these types of crimes than the ones deemed illegal. Things like corporate fraud, and bankrupting millions. The mortgage crisis where executives made millions and left millions in despair. Things like the legal manufacturing of narcotics and health debilitating substances. Let me add environmental crimes, including climate, which adversely affect millions of lives. These of course would depend on your definition of a crime.

Last quick thing. What about war? What is it good for? Absolutely nothing! Is war a crime? Is collateral damage a crime? Is war for financial gain a crime? Is war for the benefit of trade, political favors or just plain anger, a crime? What does Christianity have to do with war or this book? Wars justified for profit. Wars fought claiming to save a philosophy. Wars that result in thousands of collateral casualties. Wars that are sold to the public base on lies. Are we Christians? Do we follow the teachings of Jesus? Many wars can be traced back to our devotion to economic gain, inequality all raped up in a bunch of lies. It just so happens the Old Testament contains fifty seven wars. The New Testament one. There was the destruction of Jerusalem, but hardly a battle. There is no justification for evangelical, bible-believing Christians to justify starting a war. If America is attacked, yes, I agree. Should we have protected ourselves when Pearl Harbor was destroyed? Yes. After September 11th, 2001. Yes. Just should have been the right country. Do I think the Jewish community should have waged war on Hitler? I do. But they did not. Blessed are the peacemakers and those who mourn.

So after all the talk about policies, I am sure many are stretching their necks and rolling their eyes, thinking politics and religion are two different things. Hooray, ya'll are right. What should we be upholding and living to achieve? What should our principles emulate? The right, the left or God? Should be a simple answer to a simple question. But our world has distorted our purpose as human beings and really warped our thinking of what policies we should support. A nations policies should be enacted to preserve the well being of the citizens of the nation and the land on which they live. Though Christianity may not be directly to blame for America's high crime ra tes its interpretation and lack of adherence to Christian ideology definitely plays a huge part.

During our history, the United States has expanded its territory through many un-Christian like behavior. Should we re-hash the genocide and slaughter across the globe. In addition, we have sided with countries, aided, supplied weapons or supplied funds to countries based on a multitude of reason, but only one goal or philosophy which on the two words was political and economic. War and choses of side seem to always benefit our interest, our growth, or just fulfill a self- justified goal. All these acts exemplified Christianity, in America.

As a nation we seemingly claim to have enough "chips" to unjustly do what we want to certain countries. And it has not only been like that since the end of the 1st World War and 2nd World War but upheld on many occasions by the United States, as one of the "families", sometimes playing the role of crime families. As a nation we would define and dictate what would be globally recognized treaties, agreements, boundaries and the way forward for the majority of the world. Jesus spoke of the wars of the future. He said that nation would rise against nation and kingdom against kingdom and that Judaea would be destroyed, Jerusalem besieged and taken by the gentiles, and the Temple defiled and destroyed. Well I have a question, who are the Gentiles? In all the wars and destruction of civilizations who were the ones destroyed and what characteristic did all of them share? Those professing to be Christian, those false prophets and those not respecting and being kind to all God's creations are the ones whom will pay the price. Before I wrap up this section, I want to discuss the highest court in the land. The Supreme Court. What does the statement, "the highest court in the land", mean to you and to the rest of the world? The Supreme Court was formed to be the final decider of how equal justice, civil rights and liberties would be upheld. It is also supposed to protect citizens by over-turning or striking down laws that violate the Constitution. There are a few things I want to point out. Upholding an unjust constitution in itself perpetuates inequality and injustice. The Supreme Court is supposed to be unbiased and remove all personal interest from decisions. If this were so, it should be void of any party affiliation. If the member's goals were to be the purveyors of justice, party affiliation wouldn't matter. If all the Supreme Court Justices are supposed to be Christian, equal justice should matter. Now I know the Supreme Court is constitutionally obligated to support the Constitution regardless of its applicability or common sense, but it can be amended. The problem with amending the Constitution is it has to be put in motion and approved by congress. Throughout history congress will not amend unjust laws unless people are beat, jailed or assassinated. The Supreme Court and the Federal government represents our country. They define our nation. Unlike the people in the Bible and the few men of our time who died for the belief in equality and fairness, out leaders are afraid to lose their popularity, their way of life and their votes. I am afraid that in the eyes of God they represent our nation. I could say a lot more but I will move on.

Now that we have explored the Bible, the history of world religion, the perspective of religion in the United States and the probability of Jesus coming back, do you think Jesus is happy with His legacy? Has our political and economic structure lived up to the teachings, wishes and commands of Jesus? Or has our countries legacy been built on wealth and fear.

The Far right claims that their values are constantly under attack and that at any moment everything they care about in life can be gone. Their base is completely drenched in the fear of them losing their rights. But what rights are those? The right to treat everyone with dignity and respect? But then isn't that the best way to keep people in check—through fear? Fear can be paralyzing. Honestly, fear is probably the most powerful emotion. It can render people to such a state of mental instability that all rational thought and logic fly right out the window. Which, for Far right Republicans, is a great thing. How could someone state "if he looses, there will be violence"? How could the leader of a Christian nation stir up fear wrongly characterizing the morals and life styles of a nation? How could the leader of a Christian nation approve of fascist beliefs?

What can we do as Christians to honor the teachings of Jesus and the Word of God? Do we re-evaluate how we live and the morality lost? Do we simply start living and conducting all facets of our lives as Christians should? Do we change our political and/ or economic structure? And what would that mean to change our economic structure in a way that exemplified Christianity?

If we offered programs to protect our children, elderly, citizens and planet would that make us Socialist, as Republicans claim? Now correct me if I am wrong Socialism is a political economical governmental structure. It is not a religious sect or even view. For that reason Christians who argue a Christian country should not enact a program because it is viewed as socialist needs to do their homework. The two have nothing to do with each other politically. I would state, for those who feel capitalism is closer to Jesus teachings than socialism to go back and read the bible and take some political science courses.

The free education, health and elderly care provided by Democratic Socialist countries is to be admired. For all the far-right readers who say, "See, he wants our country to a socialist" Or, he's a socialist commie" First you are an idiot. That is not what I am saying. We just have to be Christ- like. And if that means adopting Christ like behaviors that are comparable to socialist views, then so be it. We must remember, understand and take heed. Jesus did not start a religion. Man did. Jesus is the religion. Some of our founding fathers knew what man would do to religion and the affects it would have on America. Let us not even mention that Revelation was prophesized based on us not following His word. Yeah some argue America is far better than other countries. And once again, most of those countries are not "Christian". They are Third World. So that's a bad standard to compare ourselves.

When we take in all the knowledge of the Bible. Meaning the actual entire Bible, not individual verses. When we look at the history of Christianity and when we hear the things that come out of the mouths of supposedly men of God and our so-called leaders, we should, with intelligence, wisdom and discernment conclude one thing. There may be many Christians in America, but our country has not lived up to what she preaches.

Conclusion

Now that we are coming to the end of the book let me do a quick recap and then reflect on my original thoughts and purpose of writing this book. Throughout the Bible there is a constant message of love, loyalty, redemption and faith of God's word and Jesus messages. A simple message. Simplistically put, do the right thing! Treat each other with love and respect. Do as the one you believe in, taught. If that is Jesus, do what He said to do. Act like He said you should act. Love as He said you should love. I have stated many Christians are wonderful human beings. As are Muslims, Jews and atheist. So why focus on Christianity? Because of the hypocrisy of many of our leaders and hypocrisy of many calling themselves Christians. My original focus was on former President Trump as he was the current POTUS when I began writing. As things played out, I took notice of the far right Republicans and seventy five million plus persons who supported him. I asked myself, could it be possible that Trump is just the vehicle using the faults, prejudices and hatefulness of the American people. And throughout history there is a name associated for those who galvanize people to believe or act unjustly, illegally and immorally. If that is true then I was more on track than originally thought. It is an American issue. It is the problem of a nation who professes to be Christian. And our leaders who claim to be the most "Christian ever". Which is pure insanity. Our leaders who claim their favorite book is the Bible but could not tell you one complete chapter in the entire book. Our leaders who claim others are not Christian and do not even understand the consequences of saying that about someone and bearing false witness against someone. Our leaders who take pictures holding a Bible moments after ordering inhumane treatment of peaceful protesters. Citizens who claim to be Christian, but have no problem committing acts of insurrection and domestic terror. First of all that act of taking a picture is a way of taken the

Lord's name in vain. But many won't even understand that. So my premise is how can someone say we need to get back to our Christian foundation and live worse than the Roman rulers or any other ruler of a nation that dishonored God at every turn.

Throughout our history, racial and ethnicity divides have been prevalent long before our understanding and acceptance of religion. It is this divide, that can be defined in the terms of or traced back to each of our DNA and upbringing. Our desire to know, understand and accept that which the Bible teaches is understood and twisted base on who we are or whom we choose to be. There is a small exception that view spirituality in terms of faith. But though these should be the norm they are the exceptions. Remember I posed two questions throughout this book to be pondered. One is, was America founded on Christian principles. The main question was, is America a Christian nation? Not does America have the most Christians? Is America's population living up to teaching and wishes of Jesus? Is it safe to say at this point in our history Jesus is weeping? Or, is Jesus sitting back feeling pleased that His word has engulfed our spirit and manifest itself through our everyday lives. We need to emphatically understand if He is weeping it is not because of the acts of Muslims, Mexicans, Black or the LGBT community. If He is weeping it is because of all the hate, vanity, selfishness, loathing, and narcissism and racism. If He is weeping it is because of all the words He taught were in vain.

I tried to tell the story from the beginning. I wanted everyone to understand from the Bible, all throughout history, man, for some reason has never been all in with God. We have looked at scripture, American history and current policies. Sure, we have taken scripture and teachings, and adopted beliefs to make ourselves feel good about ourselves and parade around like we are holier than thou. But, our history, economic system, prejudices and policies tell a different story. Our country was willfully and very strategically founded. Our government was framed to provide latitude for the lawmakers and the citizens alike. That latitude though carefully planned and designed to prevent the government from having too much power inadvertently resulted in loop-holes, inequality and generations caught in a cycle of despair and uncertainty. The sad thing is, that we are not Christian or even spiritual enough to realize that others doubt who our nation is. There are others that just feel superior because they call themselves Christian. What do you think Jesus feels? Do you think He looks at the state of our country and is debating against revelation and the apocalypse?

Man's connection to a higher, supreme power began long before the divisions of religion. The divisions that were birthed from power, selfishness, politics, capitalism and domination. So, I ask everyone. Which of those resemble the life or teaching of Jesus? Jesus is clearly frustrated and perhaps even offended by people who seem not to know what it means to be His follower or what it means to be a disciple, or what good thing one can do for the world on behalf of the many. Many may ask God or even a pastor, "What must I do so that I will have eternal life?" I feel Jesus has not only repeatedly answered that question, but is unsatisfied with many of the answers now given. You cannot recite something or give "Hail Mary's" to get into Heaven. Many say to be a Christian is to understand these things and to know who we are in Christ. I say we first need to know who Christ was. Who we are as Christians? And why Jesus teachings are so important to our lives. When we look at the premise of Christianity, which is the New Testament, we have to strive to obtain a world or country that lives up to what Jesus taught. We are a nation divided by race, politics, and socio-economic factors. Many people turn a blind eye to racism, to pedophilia, to intolerance of all kinds. Let me state unequivocally that there are caring doctors, Christian or not, whom serve the poor, who live modestly. There are lawyers who set up practice in low-income neighborhood. There are priest and pastors who continue ministering in the same community church, live in their tasteful home and some on church grounds. There are humble persons living lives of service and giving. There are those who help i the nderprivileged. Those in need. You get it. I guess this book wasn't for everyone after all! You are appreciated.

Why do many Christians choose what scripture they will follow? Most choose scripture that are either in line with their respective pastors or justify their un-Christian like far right views. Every Christian denomination has a different twist on what is the truth and what they deem as wrong or un-Christian. They base it on a ritualistic act or one particular scripture interpretation. But it is clearly written. Do what is right. For God, for Jesus, for humanity. It used to be, just do what is right. The lines of right and wrong have been blurred. Politics, legalities and religion blurred these lines. So I would suggest doing what we're supposed to do. If you claim to be a Christian do what you are supposed to do according to the Word of God.

"Many will say to Me in that day, 'Lord, Lord, have we not prophesied in Your name, cast out demons in Your name, and done many wonders in Your name?' "And then I will declare to them, 'I never knew you; depart from Me, you who practice lawlessness! Matthew 7:22 KJV.

My question is if you claim to be a Christian, "does Jesus know you?" Do you know yourself?

For so long I despised Catholics for condoning slavery, child abuse and gathering wealth and power. As I stated I am not a Catholic, but then I saw a Pope who denounced un-Godly behavior. I saw a Pope who practiced Christianity, not just yapped. I saw a Pope who washed the feet of the poor. Stood up against pedophilia and gave away the inherent riches that came with the office and embraced the people. He was actually pro vaccine. I am actually surprised by how many American Catholics talk bad about him. Do you know why many despise him? Maybe because he is trying to live according to the tenets of the Bible. Sure he still has to do what Popes do. And there are things that are institutional and will probably never change. Let me be repetitive. Washed a man's feet! That wasn't the Catholic way

I knew growing up.. And it sure ain't the American Christian way. Oh, I still am not a Catholic, but the new Pope is at least is trying to be a Christian. Or maybe he is not trying to be a Christian or Catholic. Maybe he is trying to be true to Jesus. As true as allowable.

Many in our country still embrace the powerful and hierarchical empire. The wealthy and over achievers, the brash, bold arrogant narcissist. The Bible clearly teaches us Gods' expectation, to not only follow his laws but more importantly to be mindful or aware of His tone.

Sometimes people ignore and even berate those who say they are not Christian, when they speak of tolerance and love. By today's standards of how society defines Christianity, maybe that's a good thing. So hold your head high. Let me state unequivocally that there are caring people, Christian or not, whom serve the poor, who live modestly. Let me repeat myself. There are lawyers who set up practice in low-income neighborhood. There a priest and pastors who continue ministering in the same community church, live in their tasteful simple home on church grounds. There are humble persons living lives of service and giving. You get it. Again.

So my question to all the readers. What do you think a Christian is? Let me help you. Is a Christian someone who lives as Moses or Jesus? Trick question. Is a Christian someone who would wash a homeless man's feet or laugh and mock him? Is a Christian someone who believes in giving his money once a week to an institution? Or someone who feeds the hungry and poor? If Jesus walked in todays' world, would He be the one in the suit or the one in the jeans? What about wealth? Did Jesus teach that the desire to achieve wealth would help or hinder one obtaining heavenly gifts? Note, there is a huge difference in seeking wealth and gaining wealth. If Jesus walked the earth today would He be eating caviar, dining with the rich or sitting besides the homeless sharing a meal? A Christian is someone who lives like Jesus did and would. Or, at least strives to with all his/her heart and soul.

A Christian is someone who though may not physically live like Jesus did but could and would. Is a Christian someone who goes to church every Sunday, sings in the choir but then shoots and unarmed human being in the back? According to the scripture, the words in the Bible, not man's opinion or interpretations, would Jesus be more of a Republican, Democrat, Communist, Socialist or White Nationalist. Would He believe that Black Lives Matter? Of course he would. Would he associate himself with Catholicism, Evangelism, Baptist, Islam or just be Spiritual. Maybe He wouldn't be any of those. Why would he need to be? Why are we?

Many people in the world feel if you lie, but it cannot be proven, that it is not a lie. To those I emphatically state. "You have not read the Bible" That is not scripture. As a matter of fact, to the contrary, scripture sites the affects of those who lied and cheated (never got caught). But suffered severe and dire consequences. So many persons in the government need to repent, run and hide, beg for forgiveness and start telling the truth. Tell me Bible readers… Who will judge you on the lie you so brilliantly pulled off and got away with? To be honest many of the people I know, think a lie is determined on proof. Really!? Just like you didn't commit a crime just because you got away with it. And why so many of them that claim they go to church or listen to their favorite TV pastor, believe they are not lying if the victim does not have proof or worse accepts or succumb to the lies.

If the word and interpretations you followed, was from the White House, Fox News, TV evangelist or other hustlers and pimps you are being taught false and misrepresentations of God's word. Remember the chapters and Books of the Bible that harp on and repeatedly warn us of false prophets. And, remember at some point we will be judged or at least asked, why did we listen to lies?

Let go back to discuss our Nation. So what about our great nation? I am asking the reader. I already have my answer to that question. Maybe you had time to think about this. List all the reasons our country is great. What did you list? Our wealth, technology, armed forces? Maybe you listed democracy. We could take a chapter on how democracy is defined. We could also discuss the events in our history that occurred for our democracy to take shape. We could also argue that for millions of people there is no true democracy. But we won't. I will assume you read this book and already know this. I assume you watch television. I assume you already know that our politicians and their supporters have down and continue to do things to subvert democracy. What I will say is I do not think we have established our greatness because of the way we treat the poor, the elderly, the disabled, the environment or just about anyone or anything. Maybe our greatness is our constitution or the second amendment and the right to bear arms. I am not sure if we have obtained the title of the greatest country because how we treat the environment, our allies or our stand and fight for the values Jesus tried so hard to put in each of our hearts. Maybe your answer to why our nation is great is that we are Christian. If so, state your case according to the scripture. I emphatically mean the scripture. Not what you heard from someone in church, on the television, from your grandpappy and not even me. The facts is what the facts are. What I mean by state your case, is what do you feel makes us a Christian nation? I am not being funny or facetious. Here is your moment to teach me. Give me knowledge. What Biblical, historical or confirming event makes us as a nation Christian? Maybe I should change my question to why do you think we are a Christian nation, what would your answer be? Because we say we are, or because it is about money? Maybe after reading this book you still think people fled Europe to practice Christianity or you will feel our founding fathers were all Christian and had the best interest of Native Americans or slave. Could it really be because we live in a country that exemplifies Jesus nature throughout the world? Do we put people before our selfishness? Yes, does the world look at us as the great power or the great Christian nation?

One thing is for sure. If you travel to other countries you should ask the citizens of those respective nations.

Has being a Christian nation kept us from having one of the highest infant mortality death rates? Has being a Christian nation saved the lives of the elderly, the homeless and unarmed citizens? Has being a Christian nation prevented gun violence, mass murders and homegrown terrorists? Has being a Christian nation kept us from having the highest amount of Covid-19 related deaths? Has being a Christian nation encouraged political leaders to put God first as oppose to their political party or political goals?

Do you have any idea to whom God and Jesus gave the many lessons, instructions, blessings and admonishment? Have you ever thought why Revelation is in the bible, why it exist at all and who it is referencing? What happens in the Middle East, terrorist activity or even Russia will not bring Revelation to fruition. What happens in the United States of America will. Why? Because we raised our hand and stuck out our chest. The inhumane, unjust acts of the self-professed "Christian Nation", the greatest country in the world is what will be the doom of mankind. As told, it will be the false prophets that puts things in motion. Is it too late? It will be those who were blessed to know and teach the truth who will ultimately set in motion, what is prophesized to happen. Apologies if I sound like the bearded guy with the cardboard sign yelling, "The End is Near". Nah I am just someone putting all the facts together with hope we can truly get a reprieve.

As a nation and a leader, we show the world that we support inhumane, racist, fraudulent, behavior. We not only support, but we have enacted laws making it legal to kill unarmed citizens. We have enacted laws where a leader can do or say anything inappropriate, politically incorrect, racist, womanizing and get a pass because it was constitutional. We have no excuse for neglecting the poor, the widows, the orphans, the disabled, the homeless, and others who are pushed to the fringe of society.

Remember I started off saying "This book is for the believers and unbelievers. Notice that the Old Testament verses are not written to unbelievers in the world, but to the nation of Israel, Judah, and in the strictest sense, the people of God. Far right, evangelical Christians in America 'spend more time in the persecution of others than in being persecuted.

I guess the man who poses with Bible, proclaims the Bible is his favorite book, never denounces racist beliefs, doesn't honor women, has no love for the LBGT, shows no respect for third world peoples, shows no loyalty to allied countries and just refuses to care about humanity. I guess this man knows his fate according to the book he loves most. This is not my opinion, my judgement or my feelings. This is what we as Christian and as any spiritual person should know to be facts.

The good news is that those who suffer great wrongs on earth are promised great rewards in heaven. So I guess if you believe this then you should know if you will receive great riches. If not read the book again. Better yet, read the Bible, probably for the first time.

If Jesus is going to return where do you think that place will be? And when that day comes, do you think he will be proud and happy about how we honored His name?

Let me be clear and attempt to articulate the truth. Not all far-right disrespect Christianity or the values of true spiritualism. Not all Democrats, Socialist or any other political groups or factions are Christian. But we should be intelligent, aware and loyal to the tenets of Christianity and humanity and make sure whoever leads our country does exhibit these characteristics. Truth, humanity, equality and justice should not be a partisan issue or mandate. Remember there are still millions of Americans who don't believe in justice for all. There a still millions of Americans who believe only in equality for those like them. There are still millions of Americans and thousands whom still hold public office, that feel they have no duty to ensure that life, liberty and the pursuit of happiness is a right to all human beings. We must make sure that whoever is in office that all government officials help define what our country claims to be. From President, to senators, congress representatives, governors, mayors and councilpersons all must adhere to, support and defend every man's rights and every man's opportunity to live and prosper. Our leaders should ensure every man's right not to get shot in the back or while sleeping.

If we want Jesus to smile and to have mercy on us all, we must remember.

True Christians may lie, but they are not liars

True Christians aren't pedophiles and do not molest children

True Christians do not hate other races, other ethnicities

True Christians are not narcissistic hypocrites

True Christians would not belittle other Christians and side with Dictators

True Christians do not go around killing unarmed citizens

True Christians do not tweet hate… all night long

True Christians would not make, market and sell pharmaceuticals that cause deaths.

True Christians do not disparage persons with different or opposing views

True Christians would not order or approve the separation and confinement of babies, infants and children.

True Christians would not willfully destroy God's earth.

The truth is good human beings do not do those things, No matter what political or religious affiliation.

And one more thing. Real Christians don't pose in front of a church holding a Bible.

I believe a Christian nation would never condone those things. How do I know these things? Because I read the Bible and the words of Jesus.

Truth, equality, democracy and justice are key staples of a Christian body and nation. Truth, equality, democracy and justice should be the key stables of good human beings regardless of religious beliefs or lack thereof.

Poverty, inequality, and self-consuming wealth are the attributes of a non-Christian nation. Again, this book is food for thought. I admit I seek the finer things in life. But we must understand, I must understand, that I cannot fit through the eye of a needle.

When it comes time to make political choices and alliance please do not choose based on partisan views, and please do not choose based on your continuing loyalty to one whose views are mutually exclusive to the basic principles of Christianity and basic spirituality. Please do choose based on your moral and spiritual convictions. Please make sure your political choices are based on humane principals, just principles, Christian principles and spiritual principals. Whosoever may be the current incumbent make sure they support and fight for humanity, equality and justice for all.

When I do the math, the cause and effect, develop and hypothesis and draw a conclusion, I analyze these facts. We are a democratic nation, we are a professed Christian nation. Therefore we should align with countries with similar belief systems. We generally define democratic nation as one where the people choose their governing legislators, or the authority to decide on legislation. But we align with countries based on the possibility of benefits, goods and services. We spent billions and less in lives to protect and attempt to convince other countries to become democratic. As of today we accomplished that in many regions around the world. But what have we shown the world?

Other countries do not hate the United States because we are a Christian nation. They hate us because we are not...what we claim to be.